By and For
The People

By and For The People

Building an Advanced Socialist Society in Bulgaria

Edited by Marilyn Bechtel

NWR Publications, Inc.
New York, N.Y.

335. 4977
B99

RK

NWR Publications, Inc.
156 Fifth Avenue
New York, N.Y. 10010
1977

Library of Congress Catalog Card Number:
76-62559

ISBN: 0-916972-01-1
Printed in the U.S.A.

 209

CONTENTS

A Land Transformed in One Generation
    MARILYN BECHTEL 7

Bulgaria and Socialist Mutual Assistance
    CLAUDE M. LIGHTFOOT 19

Report to the 11th Congress of the
Bulgarian Communist Party
    TODOR ZHIVKOV 25

Closing Remarks
    TODOR ZHIVKOV 137

Notes 142

MARILYN BECHTEL

A Land Transformed
In One Generation

A small country of great contrasts, from the rugged forested mountains of the Balkan Range to the golden sands of the Black Sea coast, Bulgaria counts its riches both in fertile farmland and in the mineral wealth needed for industry. The People's Republic of Bulgaria is today a beautiful and prosperous country with a rapidly developing industrial-agricultural economy and a full, multifaceted cultural, educational and recreational life.

To appreciate fully the significance of the Bulgarian people's accomplishments, it is essential to remember that a hundred years ago, Bulgaria was a harshly oppressed province of a decadent, failing but still powerful Ottoman Empire. For nearly seven decades after the achievement of independence in 1878, Bulgaria remained a poverty-stricken agricultural hinterland. It was not until after the Socialist Revolution of September 9, 1944 that the transformation of Bulgaria began.

The common people's constant struggle against their various oppressors is a sturdy thread running throughout Bulgarian history. During the sixth and seventh centuries, as part of the vast migration of peoples that reshaped Europe, several Slavic tribes settled on the Balkan

MARILYN BECHTEL became Editor of NEW WORLD REVIEW on January 1, 1977.

7

peninsula south of the Danube. The Bulgarian Kingdom was founded in 681, based on the alliance of these tribes with a recently-arrived Turkic people, the Proto-Bulgarians. As Bulgaria developed into a powerful state, the ensuing centuries were filled with conflicts with the neighboring Byzantine empire. Development of the Slavonic alphabet by the scholars Cyril and Methodius in the mid-ninth century paved the way for the country to become a major center of medieval scholarship, literature and art.

This flowering of culture, however, failed to benefit the common people, who bore the burden of constant wars, oppressive taxes and forced labor. As a consequence, Bulgaria became the birthplace of Bogomilism, a popular protest movement in the form of a religious heresy. The Bogomils rejected the authority of nobles and established church as created by an "impure force." Aided by tight organization and a popular literature, they built a mass movement whose fighting force shook the foundations of the kingdom. The movement spread throughout southern Europe, being known in France as the Albigenses and in Italy as the Cathari.

Meanwhile the Bulgarian state expanded and contracted according to the fortunes of its struggles with Byzantium and with invading tribes, the consolidation or disintegration of its feudal relations, and the pressures exerted by its struggling peoples. For 170 years of the eleventh and twelfth centuries, it was dominated by the Byzantine Empire. The Second Bulgarian Kingdom which followed was marked by constant turmoil, including the brief accession to the throne in 1277 of Europe's only peasant-king, the swineherd Ivailo. This period was also a time of outstanding cultural advances, when architecture, religious literature, painting and crafts flourished with great brilliance.

Internally divided, constantly warring with each other, the neighboring Balkan states were easy prey to the Turkish incursions of the late 1300s. The last Bulgarian territory was conquered in 1396, beginning five long centuries of brutal oppression.

Isolated, severely exploited, relentlessly taxed and compelled to perform labor service, driven from towns and fertile land, subject to humiliating discrimination, sold into slavery, exiled, forced in many places to convert to Islam—such was the lot of Bulgarians under the Ottoman Empire. They never ceased to struggle. Among the many forms of resistance was the *haidouk* movement of guerrilla bands in the mountains. Uprisings occurred constantly—some urban, some rural, some staged by small groups of plotters, and others on a mass scale. From the 17th century on, these intensified, as decay and acute financial crisis gripped the Ottoman Empire.

The Empire's difficulties opened new economic and cultural opportunities. Better-off Bulgarians began to buy land. Participation in European trade stimulated specialized production in agriculture and crafts. Thus began the National Revival of the 18th and 19th centuries. Along with the struggle to regain the independence of the Bulgarian Church, which was controlled by the Greek patriarchate, a powerful movement for secular culture sprang up and a strikingly beautiful national style of architecture developed.

The catalyst of the revival was the monk Paissy of Hilendar. His *History of the Slav-Bulgarians*, finished in 1762, passed hand-to-hand in secret, spreading knowledge of the national heritage and pointing the way to a new level of political struggle. By the 19th century, secu-

9

lar primary and secondary schools replaced the rudimentary "cell" schools of earlier centuries. Bulgarian literature flourished, theater and periodicals began to emerge.

In the changing conditions of the mid-19th century, outstanding revolutionary leaders emerged, including Georgi Sava Rakovski, Vassil Levski, Hristo Botev and Georgi Benkovski. The April 1876 uprising was the climax of the long struggle against the Turks, the largest and most widespread rebellion. Though it failed, it led directly to the Russian intervention which secured autonomy for much of Bulgaria in 1878.

The late 19th century was a time of considerable industrial growth, and of the most oppressive conditions for the emerging Bulgarian working class. The working people, true to their centuries-old tradition of struggle, saw their own interests with increasing clarity. In 1891, Dimiter Blagoev founded the Bulgarian Social-Democratic Party (later the Communist Party), which grew steadily and provided strong leadership to the developing trade union movement. When in 1904 the various unions joined in the General Workers Trade Union, a young printer named Georgi Dimitrov was elected to its leadership. The end of the 19th century also saw the founding of the Bulgarian Agrarian Union, the party of the farmers.

The year after World War I broke out, Bulgaria joined the Central Powers led by Germany. The opposition parties sided with the Entente, and only the Social-Democrats declared against the war. As the fortunes of the Central Powers waned, Bulgaria experienced economic ruin, loss of land and untold human suffering. Revolts and soldiers' mutinies rocked the land and echoes of the Russian Revolution struck a responsive chord. The people would

10

no longer permit the old parties to govern, and in 1919, Alexander Stamboliyski, head of the Bulgarian Agrarian Union, formed a new government. The BAU introduced a number of significant measures including partial land reform and a progressive income tax.

The Agrarians, however, thought that their majority in the national legislature would allow them to fight both the reactionaries and the Communists. Stamboliyski ignored the Communists' repeated warnings of impending disaster, and when the reactionaries overthrew the government in 1923, he was assassinated along with several other ministers and legislators. A fascist government now ruled.

The heroic but unsuccessful September 1923 uprising organized by the Bulgarian Communist Party was the world's first attempt by progressive forces to halt the onslaught of fascism. In the years that followed, Bulgarian fascism advanced and receded. From 1931 to 1934, for instance, a somewhat less repressive regime included BAU representatives. During this time a number of districts sent Communists to the legislature at every election, only to have the government annul the results. In 1931, the Communists won the municipal elections in Sofia. Had not the national government invalidated the results, Sofia would have been the first capital city of a capitalist country to have a Communist mayor and municipal council majority.

One of the most outstanding instances of the Communists' resistance was the heroic role of Georgi Dimitrov at the Reichstag Fire trial of 1933. Turning the tables completely on his accusers, Dimitrov gained the attention of the entire world with his brilliant attack on fascism. World opinion forced his release, but he was not allowed to return to Bulgaria until after the Nazis were defeated.

As World War II approached, Bulgaria, beneath a "neutral" cover, inched closer and closer to Nazi Germany. Finally in March 1941 the Bulgarian government joined the Axis powers. Shortly thereafter, Nazi troops entered the country.

The people, however, maintained their staunch opposition to fascism and war. The BCP worked vigorously to fan resistance in solidarity with the other conquered Balkan peoples. It brought together the Bulgarian antifascist forces in the Fatherland Front, an organization which played a central role in the postwar period, and continues to have important tasks in socialist times. A large and well-organized partisan movement spread throughout the country. The success of the popular resistance is shown by the fact that not a single Bulgarian Jew was turned over to the Nazi extermination camps, Bulgaria never declared war on the USSR, and was the only country occupied by German fascists that did not send one of its soldiers to the Eastern Front.

As the Red Army advanced, Bulgaria's liberation was assured. The Central Committee of the BCP gave the signal to take power from the bourgeois government and a nationwide uprising followed. On the night of September 8, 1944, the Bulgarian freedom fighters occupied key posts in Sofia and arrested the fascist leaders. The September 9 Uprising was in fact Bulgaria's socialist revolution. The Fatherland Front government immediately entered the war, and Bulgarian troops assisted greatly in freeing their Balkan neighbors.

Following the popular referendum and elections of September and October 1946, Bulgaria became a republic and the Bulgarian Workers' Party (Communists) under the leadership of Georgi Dimitrov, won an impressive majority. Thus the path was cleared for the development of the modern, socialist Bulgaria of today, and the complete transformation of the life of the people.

Like the rest of Eastern Europe, Bulgaria emerged from the Second World War with its industrial and agricultural resources depleted or destroyed, and faced a great problem of reconstruction even to return to prewar levels of production.

Just prior to the war, agriculture was dominant. Industry, with poorly developed textile production, food processing and coal mining, provided only a small portion of the national income. The agriculture of that time consisted of individual small farming. Cattle provided the only power, irrigation and mineral fertilizer were almost unknown. In 1975, industry accounted for just over half of the national income, and agriculture, though its output had grown two and a half times, provided less than a quarter.

In 1947, industries, mines and banks were nationalized and state monopoly over foreign trade was established. All means of production became the property of the people, and planned development of the economy was begun. The Soviets provided great economic assistance. In agriculture, the transition to cooperative farms was complete by 1958, and many state farms had been established. Extensive merging of cooperative farms in 1958 and 1959 made possible great increases in production. A further transition is taking place now, to agro-industrial complexes involving development of market and technical crop specialization on vast land areas, huge poultry factory farms, pig-breeding factories, and industrial dairy farms. Ultimately these will be linked directly with processing factories. Not only does this development greatly increase efficiency of production, but it also makes it possible to overcome the difference between town and

13

country life, between factory and farm work.

Thanks also to mechanization, use of chemicals and irrigation, Bulgaria now outranks the US, Canada and Italy in average wheat yield per unit of land, and ranks high in Europe in corn yield. Farm production is now nearly three times greater than in the best prewar year, and labor productivity has quintupled. Vegetables and fruit including grapes rank high among agricultural products, and Bulgaria is a leading producer of prize-winning wines.

In industry, the past three decades have seen the development of whole new branches including machine building, metallurgy, chemical production, and a wide variety of consumer goods. This rapid growth has been made possible by the great amount of assistance from the Soviet Union, as well as by the increasing cooperation among the socialist countries belonging to the Council of Mutual Economic Assistance (CMEA). Output of the engineering industry has increased 477 times, of the chemical industry almost 300 times, metallurgy 330 times and power generation about 80 times.

Bulgarian industry now ranks fourth in the world and second in Europe in production of electric and internal combustion engine trucks, fifth in copper sulfate, tenth in heavy trailers for trucks. Other important products include hoists and cranes, electronic products, and ships including 100,000 tankers.

About two million tons of pig iron and steel are produced yearly, as well as rolled metal, alloy steel, pipes and sheet iron. Non-ferrous metals include lead, zinc, copper and silver products. Aluminum parts and foil will soon be added. The chemical industry meets nearly all the country's needs for motor fuel and oil, produces synthetic rubber, a variety of plastics, chemical and min-

14

eral fertilizers. A very extensive pharmaceutical industry is noted for compounds to treat the after-effects of polio, heart disease and intestinal problems.

Power production, which used to depend on water and coal, has included atomic power stations since 1974, and it is planned that by the end of the century such plants will provide more than half Bulgaria's power.

Light industry emphasizes textiles, leather goods and footwear, glass and porcelain, and quality food products. Tobacco processing is important.

Bulgaria's trading partners include 110 nations. Heading her export list are machines and equipment including complete plant installations (35 per cent) and agricultural products, raw or processed (over 40 per cent).

All this has meaning because it provides the base on which the lives of individual Bulgarian people have changed totally in the time of one generation. Behind the figures on increasing production lie the figures on increasing income: since 1956 real per capita income has risen an average of 6.4 per cent a year, and in 1973 this increased to 7.6 per cent. In 1972, per capita real income was over three times that of 1952, and the increase has been most marked among the cooperative farmers and the lower paid workers.

Over 60 per cent of the housing now in use was built under socialism—more than 1.3 million units in this country of 8.7 million. The problem is not regarded as solved yet, and accelerated construction is planned. Another contrast—in 1944 only 30 per cent of the people lived in houses with electricity. Now it is universal.

All Bulgarian people benefit in myriad ways from the public funds which support health care, education, old age and disability pensions, cultural, sport and leisure activities. Bulgarians have historically known that education was essential to realizing their goals. Before the revolution, however, almost a quarter of them remained illiterate. Today the network of educational facilities assures everyone a quality education. Starting with kindergartens which now accommodate two-thirds of the children between 3 and 7, facilities include primary education (grades 1 through 8), secondary education (grades 9 through 11), specialized secondary, vocational, technical and higher education. Special attention is paid to working students attending evening classes, and they receive up to 50 days of paid leave per year to prepare for their examinations. Students have the use of special medical facilities (free, as is all health care) and many vacation resorts in the mountains and on the Black Sea coast. Higher education enrollment has increased more than ten-fold over the 10,169 students of prewar times.

In health services, the revolution is even more striking. In 1944 there was one physician for over 2,000 people, and in rural areas one physician often served more than 9,000 people scattered in distant villages. The ratio of physicians is now less than 1:479, and the network of village health centers assures availability of modern medical care to everyone. Prevention is the first principle, and special attention is paid to care for expectant mothers. The Bulgarians take full advantage of their country's fine climate, seashore, and numerous mineral springs to operate an extensive list of health resorts and spas. The success of all these efforts is demonstrated in the extension of the average life span from less than 52 years before World War II, to nearly 74 for women and 68 for men.

Socialism guarantees full equality to women, and they now make up more than half the students and teachers in institutions of higher education, and among economists. Their numbers are rising in all types of work except the physically harmful, and in all areas of public activity. The Family Code provides equal rights and responsibilities for husband and wife. Leave for childbirth ranges from four months with full pay and six months at minimum wage for the first child, to six and eight months respectively for the third.

Vacations for all workers and collective farmers range from a minimum of 14 working days to as much as 35 or even 60. A five-day workweek is the norm, with shortened days for those in hazardous occupations. Men may retire at 60, women at 55, on pensions which average 70 per cent of earnings, or more for those in lower earning brackets. Bulgaria was the first country to establish pensions for farmers.

Well over a million Bulgarians now spend those vacations at regular or health resorts, campsites and other holiday accommodations. The trade unions, cooperative farmers' union and Ministry of Education arrange reduced costs for holidays. Another 675,000 Bulgarians travel outside the country on vacation, and over four million foreign tourists come to Bulgaria from Eastern and Western Europe, the US and Canada.

An extensive network of youth clubs throughout the country aims to provide young people with recreation and social gathering places, and also with opportunities to take part in amateur artistic and technical activities. The youth brigade movement under the leadership of the Dimitrov Komsomol (Young Communist) organization, has built whole towns and industrial projects, contributing greatly to the modernization of the country and to the personal development of the brigade participants.

Well over half a million Bulgarians also participate in amateur artistic activities—song and dance ensembles, choirs, orchestras, theater and folk art groups. Professional artistic activities have blossomed under socialism as well, with 53 opera and theater companies, seven symphony orchestras, and work opportunities for thousands of painters, sculptors and graphic artists.

Even the most glowing statistics cannot describe the "feel" of what life is like today in Bulgaria. The most figures can do is to show how the basis has been laid in one generation for people to live in plenty, with jobs, housing, education, food, health care and support in old age or disability assured. These figures also show us how people thus freed from constant insecurity about the fundamental physical necessities of life can go on to fulfill themselves creatively, through steadily improving job and professional skills, participating in arts and sports, recreation and leisure activities, and enjoyment of the myriad cultural opportunities within their reach.

Achievements of this magnitude take everyone's participation, a lot of planning, a lot of critical analysis, and a great deal of nationwide discussion. Just such discussion took place throughout Bulgaria in the months and weeks preceding the 11th Congress of the BCP. This analysis took place not just in the various levels of the Party, but in the trade unions, the Komsomol, cooperative farmers' union, women's, cultural and professional associations. The past was critically reviewed, and the goals and plans projected to guide developments over the coming five years. Thus, the Congress was the property of all the people. That participation was reflected in every facet of the Congress, and is expressed in its most concentrated form in the report given there by Todor Zhivkov, First Secretary of the Central Committee and President of the State Council of Bulgaria, which is reproduced in its entirety in this volume.

CLAUDE M. LIGHTFOOT

Bulgaria and Socialist Mutual Assistance

The Bulgarian People's Republic is one of the best examples of what socialism has achieved for the people. The advances made in Bulgaria have a profound meaning for the Western world, including the United States which is in the throes of a deep-going crisis, which threatens to permanently ruin the life style of the people.

Bulgaria has existed for nearly thirteen centuries. During much of that time it was under foreign domination and exploitation. For five centuries it was controlled and exploited by the sultans and nobility of the Ottoman Empire. After achieving independence in 1878, it existed for 66 years as a poor agricultural country.

But whatever the situation in the past, the last 30 years have witnessed an explosive growth in all institutions of the society for the well-being of the people. During these 30 years of socialism, it has become one of the highly developed nations in today's world.

CLAUDE M. LIGHTFOOT attended the 11th Congress of the Bulgarian Communist Party as a fraternal delegate from the CPUSA. Dr. Lightfoot is a member of the CPUSA Central Committee and Political Bureau. His books include *Racism and Human Survival*, *Ghetto Rebellion to Black Liberation*, and *Black America and the World Revolution*. He is a publicist and columnist for several Black newspapers.

This writer had an opportunity to see and learn about the new Bulgaria by attending the Eleventh Congress of the Bulgarian Communist Party as a fraternal delegate from the Communist Party, USA.

I have traveled to many socialist countries in Eastern Europe, and from year to year I have been impressed by the progress being made; but what I witnessed in Bulgaria was enough to baffle the imagination.

Bulgaria, like other socialist countries, has been developing by stages. It operates with a planned approach to almost every aspect of life. In contrast to the insecurity bred within capitalist society, the Bulgarian people can measure their progress from year to year, and have full confidence in their future. This was the atmosphere that prevailed at the Eleventh Congress of the BCP. The Congress made an evaluation of what had been achieved within the Sixth Five-Year Plan, 1970-75. It took cognizance of its weaknesses as well as its achievements, and outlined another five-year plan, the Seventh, which calls for greater progress in almost every field of endeavor.

The central feature of this plan, like all previous ones, is how to correlate and accelerate all productive processes that can make for a better material, social and cultural life for all its citizens.

The Congress revealed that in the main, most of the goals of the Sixth Five-Year Plan had been achieved. Industry's share in the national income rose from 49 per cent in 1970 to 54.6 per cent in 1975. These developments took place mainly in those industries on which technological progress and efficiency depend—the power industry including nuclear energy, chemical, machine building and electronics. The volume of agricultural production also rose 3.1 per cent per year.

Thus, a formerly backward country has become a

highly developed industrial nation in a short period of time. Such a development never took place in the relationship between the US, Western European countries, and the lands that were their colonies. For the world of imperialism, a colony exists for these purposes only: a source for raw materials, a market for manufactured goods, a source of cheap labor and high returns on capital investments. This held back industrial growth and higher living standards for three-fourths of the world.

What accounts for the magnificent achievements of the Bulgarian people? What were some of the prerequisites that made possible the transformation of a backward nation into a modern nation in a period of three decades?

No doubt the character and the willingness of the people to struggle as well as the great talents that are latent in all people were major factors; but these alone will not explain these historic advances, for as Todor Zhivkov, the outstanding leader of the Bulgarian people, stated at the Congress: "Our development was considerably hindered by difficulties of an objective nature. The economic backwardness we had inherited forced us in most cases to begin construction from scratch. The working class lacked long years of tradition; scientific and engineering cadre were insufficient; the country's natural resources and a number of other factors caused and continue to cause tensions in our development."

Based on such a background the Bulgarian people could never have made this progress unaided. In fact no people in world history have risen solely by their own efforts. It has been the interplay of social advances made by various people throughout history that has enabled some nations to march forward faster than others. In our time it is socialism which combines the strength of the many to aid and facilitate the progress of all concerned that has been the pivotal point behind these miraculous changes in Bulgaria. It was not Soviet "domination" but Soviet aid that was the enabling act. Zhivkov describes how the process began:

This change was possible because the proletariat came out on the world arena, the only class in human history which has fought for power not with the aim to substitute one class society for another, but to do away once and forever with exploitation and oppression and class division of society.

It was possible because the Great October Socialist Revolution laid the beginnings of the transition from capitalism to socialism, and the USSR, guided by the Soviet Communist Party, became the lodestar and powerful mainstay of the world communist and working class movement, of the struggles of the world proletariat for socialism.

Bulgaria shall never forget the sunny days of September 1944, the arrival of the Soviet Army at our borders, the excitement around the arches with inscriptions "Welcome Brothers!", the tears of joy in the eyes of the two nations.

We remember well our first steps after September 9, what Bulgaria was like at that time and what we were like ourselves. We can remember the first Soviet tractors in the fields of our cooperative farms. The first construction projects. The first factories. We remember the first Soviet experts, those wonderful people the Soviet Union sent to help us even though it badly needed their minds and hands to restore the ruins left after the war. We have long forgotten what it means to be starving but we remember and shall never forget the taste of bread made from Soviet wheat in those hungry postwar years.

There are still people in this world who call themselves "revolutionaries" and who are so afraid for their "independence" from the Soviet Union that, lest the bourgeoisie should accuse them of imitation, they become fully dependent on bourgeois views and show an amazing readiness to give up everything, even the revolution, even the correct path of socialist construction . . . ("The 30th Anniversary of the Victory of the

22

Socialist Revolution in Bulgaria," speech on Sept. 8, 1974.)

The Bulgarian experience shows what cooperation between socialist nations can achieve, and effectively gives the lie to the anti-Soviet propagandists who say the USSR controls Eastern Europe. It also provides a searchlight for the underdeveloped nations all over the world who are learning that socialist aid is a way station leading out of world imperialist domination. Finally, revival of cold-war rhetoric about Soviet domination is hardly going to force off the stage of history a system whose time has come.

TODOR ZHIVKOV
First Secretary, Central Committee, Bulgarian Communist
Party; President, State Council, People's Republic of Bulgaria.

TODOR ZHIVKOV

Report of the Central Committee
To the Eleventh Congress of the
Bulgarian Communist Party

March 29, 1976

Comrade delegates,
Distinguished guests to our Congress,
Five years have passed since the historic Tenth Party
Congress, the first five years after the adoption of the
Party Programme on building a developed socialist
society in the People's Republic of Bulgaria.

What have these years brought us?

The Sixth Five-year Plan of the country's socio-
economic development has been successfully   fulfilled. The nation's economy has been developing along
the road of steady intensification, of scientific and
technological progress. The working people's material
well-being has increased and their cultural level has
risen in step with the development of the economy; the
people's socio-political unity has been further consolidated, the socialist lifestyle has developed. Socialist
social relations continued to improve.

After the Tenth Congress, the new Constitution of
the People's Republic of Bulgaria was submitted for
nationwide discussion and adopted by a referendum. It
sanctioned the people's socialist gains and opened the
way for the expansion of socialist democracy and the
further all-round development of the country. The

Constitution confirmed the leading role of the Bulgarian Communist Party – the Party which throughout its history and in all its activity has proved that it has no other interests to heart than the interests of the Bulgarian working people.

During the period under review, the Bulgarian Communist Party has reaffirmed with fresh force its loyalty to Marxism-Leninism and proletarian internationalism, its ability to apply creatively and develop the Leninist principles in the building of a socialist society. The Leninist style of leadership has also found striking expression in the preparations for the present Eleventh Party Congress. Elaborated by large task forces of Party, state and economic activists and specialists, a number of documents on individual important problems of our work were discussed and adopted at plenary sessions of the Central Committee, along with the Guidelines on the Country's Socio-economic Development under the Seventh Five-year Plan. The preparations for the Eleventh Congress actually started with these documents. Submitted for nationwide discussions, they aroused a keen response. Numerous suggestions were made which have been reflected in the Congress documents or will be taken into account in working out the Seventh Five-year Plan and the comprehensive programmes on the further development of individual sectors and spheres of public life.

In the past five years the Party has been unswervingly pursuing the policy, proclaimed in the Programme, of integration with the fraternal socialist states, of ever closer and fuller rapprochement of the People's Republic of Bulgaria with the Union of the Soviet

Socialist Republics. The socialist community has further gained in strength, its influence in the world has grown.

Five years ago, at its 24th Congress, the Communist Party of the Soviet Union adopted the remarkable Peace Programme. A direct successor of Lenin's Decree on Peace and an embodiment of the Leninist principles of peaceful coexistence between states with different social systems, this programme has given a powerful impetus to the struggle of the peace-loving forces. The past five years have brought about a turn from cold war to peaceful coexistence.

The great successes scored by the Bulgarian people in economic and cultural construction, in strengthening the country's defence capability and our consistent Leninist foreign policy have enhanced the international prestige of the Party and the country. Now the People's Republic of Bulgaria is a sought-after and respected partner in international relations.

Our Party and our people still feel the tremendous impact of the 25th Congress of Lenin's great Party – the standard-bearer of mankind in the age of transition from capitalism to socialism. There is no doubt whatsoever that the brilliant report of Comrade Leonid Brezhnev and the decisions of the 25th Congress will not only become a guiding principle and inspiration for the Soviet people in the construction of a communist society, but will also deepen the faith in the future and will give new strength to the millions of honest people throughout the world, fighting against war and for freedom and independence, for democracy and social progress, for socialism.

Without a doubt the growing all-round power of

socialist Bulgaria, the prospects opening up before it, the might of the socialist community of which our country is an inseparable part and the victories of the world revolutionary movement, of the peace-loving and democratic forces – everything that is happening in Bulgaria and the world – gives us reason and the right to look to the future full of optimism and to proceed along our great path with confidence.

Allow me, comrades, on behalf of the Central Committee and on behalf of the Eleventh Congress, to express most heartfelt gratitude to the Bulgarian working class, to the workers in agriculture, to the people's intelligentsia, to the Bulgarian women and mothers, to the young men and women, to all working people who by their dedicated and inspired efforts have translated into living reality the decisions of the Tenth Congress of the Bulgarian Communist Party.

Allow me to voice our unshakable confidence that the heroic and industrious Bulgarian people, guided by their tried and tested Party, will also implement the decisions which the Eleventh Congress will take in the name of our free and happy future!

I. GLOBAL SITUATION AND THE INTERNATIONAL ACTIVITY OF THE BULGARIAN COMMUNIST PARTY

Dear comrade delegates,

If we have to define the main features of the global situation in the period between the Tenth and the Eleventh Party Congresses, we should certainly emphasize *the further shift in the balance of power in favour of peace, democracy and socialism.*

The fraternal socialist states have scored fresh major successes in all spheres of life. The socialist social system has been revealing ever more fully its all-round superiority over capitalism, and has been becoming increasingly more attractive to hundreds of millions of working people in the capitalist and developing countries.

The victory scored by the heroic Vietnamese people over the imperialist interventionists and reaction will remain a bright page in the history of mankind's struggles for freedom and socialism. After selfless struggles the peoples of Laos and Cambodia have also won their freedom. Fraternal Cuba – the first socialist state in the western hemisphere – has been confidently developing and growing stronger. The German Democratic Republic has scored a great political and diplomatic victory. The just struggle of the Korean

People's Democratic Republic for the peaceful unification of Korea is gaining international support.

The fascist regimes in Portugal and Greece have collapsed. The new states of Guinea-Bissau, Mozambique, Angola, Sao Tome and Principe have been created on the ruins of the last colonial empire.

The struggles of the working class in the capitalist countries have acquired great scope. The communist parties' influence has grown. Discontent with the existing order has been mounting among the broad masses of the people; the movement for political, economic and social changes has intensified, as has the drive towards unification of the progressive forces.

In general, comrades, to use the winged words of our immortal leader Georgi Dimitrov, the wheels of history are turning and will continue to turn till the final abolition of slavery and exploitation, till the triumph of socialism, till the triumph of communism!

The process of détente and the confirmation of the Leninist principles of peaceful coexistence between states with different social systems have been the determining trend in international relations during the period under review. This process is the result above all of the shift in the balance of power between the two opposing systems to the advantage of socialism and of the socialist states' consistent peaceful policy.

The trend of détente has been politically and legally recognized in the system of treaties and agreements between the socialist and the capitalist states. The USSR – USA agreements are of paramount importance, as they are a real step forward towards eliminating the danger of a thermo-nuclear war. The successful conclusion of the Conference on Security and Cooperation in Europe was a historic event in international life.

We have repeatedly emphasized and will do so again: the credit for the confirmation of the policy of détente goes to the hundreds of millions of people throughout the world, to the different democratic forces and movements, to the ruling circles of those capitalist countries which have adopted a realistic approach to the problems of peace and war in the modern world. The role of the states of the socialist community, which promoted the idea of the Conference and consistently worked to ensure its success, is of prime importance. However, there is one thing which is indisputable for all: *the decisive contribution to the creation and confirmation of the new climate in the world has been made by the Soviet Union, by the CPSU.* To unbiased people all over the world the peaceful offensive is associated with the name and tireless activity of Leonid Ilyich Brezhnev, Secretary General of the Central Committee of the Communist Party of the Soviet Union, a worthy representative of the Leninist school of communist leaders, the most prominent and highly esteemed political leader and statesman of our age.

From this rostrum, we, the Bulgarian communists, express once again our admiration for and gratitude to the great Party of Lenin, to the Soviet Union, to our Soviet brothers, who, in decades of struggle, have defended the socialist social system through peaceful labour and arms in hand, have made and are making the greatest, decisive contribution to the promotion of human progress in conditions of peace and security of the peoples!

Comrades,

Ever since the emergence of *the world socialist system*, the Bulgarian Communist Party has always attached prime importance to the relations of the People's Republic of Bulgaria with the fraternal socialist states. And during the period under review, too we have invariably followed this policy. An entirely new type of relations has been established between our countries and peoples, based on the identity of the social system, the unity of national and international interests, the ideology of Marxism-Leninism, the close cooperation of the leading communist parties.

We are gratified to note that our *bilateral relations* with Vietnam, the German Democratic Republic, the Korean People's Democratic Republic, Cuba, Mongolia, Poland, Romania, Hungary, Czechoslovakia and Yugoslavia have been developing dynamically.

Our Party maintains close relations with the communist parties of the socialist states. During the past five years we have held meetings and talks at various levels, including at the highest level, with all ruling communist parties. The Bulgarian Communist Party has always worked and will continue to work for the further rallying of the socialist states on the basis of Marxism-Leninism and socialist internationalism.

The main political and military alliance of the socialist community is *the Warsaw Treaty Organization*. We are opposed to the division of the world into military blocs. However, we must firmly state that so long as NATO exists, so long as the capitalist states increase their military budgets, so long as military and civil adventurists threaten us by sabre-rattling, the People's

Republic of Bulgaria, together with the other fraternal states, will continue to make its full contribution to strengthening the unity, cohesion and defence capability of the socialist community, will work for the further improvement of the Warsaw Treaty Organization as a powerful barrier to the aggressive policies of imperialism.

Our countries maintain regular bilateral and multilateral relations within the framework of the Warsaw Treaty. The sessions of the *Political Consultative Committee*, at which joint decisions are taken on the most outstanding issues of our times, play a particularly important role in this respect.

The all-round strengthening of *the Council for Mutual Economic Assistance* is also a major task of our foreign policy. Late last year the countries of the Council for Mutual Economic Assistance successfully fulfilled their socio-economic plans for the 1971-1975 period. According to preliminary data, their national income increased by 36 per cent, whereas the corresponding increase in the Common Market countries was 12 per cent. The situation is similar as regards the volume of industrial output: CMEA – 45 per cent, the Common Market – 7 per cent. In 1974 our countries accounted for one-third of the world's industrial production. The five-year plans for the 1976-1980 period open up new wide vistas. Figures speak an eloquent language: the CMEA countries are the most dynamic economic community in the world.

Cooperation between the member-states of the Council for Mutual Economic Assistance has in recent years acquired new features; it has been invested with a richer content and is gradually covering an increasing number of spheres of public life. *The Comprehensive Programme of Socialist Economic Integration has initiated a qualitatively new stage in this cooperation.* The first coordinated plan of multilateral integrational undertakings for the 1976-1980 period has also been drawn up and adopted. The problems of raw and prime materials, energy, fuel, of production specialization and cooperation, the supply of more varied and better quality foodstuffs and industrial consumer goods will increasingly be tackled jointly in future. Lenin's sagacious forecast that socialism 'is creating new, superior patterns of human community, when the legitimate needs and progressive aspirations of the working people of all nationalities will be met for the first time in international unity', is gradually being realized and will be realized. (V. I. Lenin, Works, Vol. 21, p. 26)

The Bulgarian Communist Party supports in every way the policy of deepening socialist integration, of working out and implementing long-range goal-specific programmes and will continue to make its contribution to the increase of the economic potential of our socialist community.

Comrades,

Historical experience – both past and present – strengthens our conviction that *the level of mutual relations and the strength of the unity of the socialist states are determined to the highest degree by the relations and unity of each one of them with the Union of the Soviet Socialist Republics.* That is why we focus our Party political, ideological, economic, cultural and defence activity on

34

the permanent task of strengthening and deepening fraternal Bulgaro-Soviet friendship.

During the period under review, *Bulgaro-Soviet friendship* has further developed and has been qualitatively enriched. It has been reaffirmed by the Party Programme and the new Bulgarian Constitution, and it found a striking manifestation in the visit of our Party and Government delegation to the USSR in 1972 and during the unforgettable visit which Comrade Leonid Ilyich Brezhnev paid to Bulgaria in 1973. The July 1973 Plenary Session of the CC of the BCP occupies a special place in the promotion of Bulgaro-Soviet relations, as it further elaborated and enriched the policy of ever closer rapprochement between Bulgaria and the Soviet Union.

From the rostrum of the Eleventh Congress we once again declare for all to hear: we, the Bulgarian communists, the Bulgarian working people, the entire Bulgarian people can conceive of no other road of building a developed socialist society and, subsequently, of communism in Bulgaria than shoulder to shoulder with our Soviet brothers and sisters, in conditions of the closest all-round cooperation with the Party of Lenin, in conditions of ever fuller and increasingly greater rapprochement of the People's Republic of Bulgaria with the great Union of the Soviet Socialist Republics.

From the rostrum of our Eleventh Congress we reiterate our confidence that the further development of the socialist society in the individual socialist states will lead, as Lenin foresaw, to the creation of a unified co-operative of the socialist nations, and we proclaim that we have been building and will continue to build our all-round relations with the CPSU and the USSR, with the parties and peoples of the socialist states, guided and inspired by this great historical prospect.

Comrades,

The growing apace of the world revolutionary process, the continuous upsurge of the world socialist community and the progress in international relations during the last few years are taking place in the conditions of a *further deepening of the general crisis of capitalism.*

The gravest and most serious economic crisis of capitalism since the 1929-1933 recession has developed in recent years and is still continuing. The gross national product and the volume of industrial output have been curtailed. A large part of the fixed capital is now lying idle. The prospects for international trade, as well as the trade and payments balance of the capitalist countries deteriorated sharply. The army of unemployed increased to more than 17 million. The cost of living index in the industrialized capitalist countries is rising all the time. Inflation is mounting and so is insecurity of what the future will bring.

The crisis which hit all industrialized capitalist countries simultaneously, is yet further cogent proof of the fact that the capitalist system is doomed by history. Present-day conditions have confirmed the Leninist principle that neither the militarization of the economy nor the various state-monopolistic methods of regulating the process of reproduction can help overcome the severe contradictions inherent in the capitalist system. These contradictions – the contradictions between labour and capital, between the majority of the nation and the financial-monopolistic oligarchy, between the individual monopolies, and between the individual imperialist states – will grow stronger and will lead to a further erosion of the internal and international positions of capitalism. At the same time the contradictions between the imperialist states and the developing countries are being further exacerbated. The attempts being made by the imperialist states to shift the burden of the current crisis onto the economies of the third world countries is encountering their growing and increasingly united opposition on the international arena. The movement of the non-aligned states is gaining momentum as an anti-imperialist force.

Against the background of the deepening of the general crisis of capitalism *the positions of the working class and of its communist vanguard are growing stronger and their role is expanding.* A powerful offensive against the monopolies and imperialist reaction is growing apace. Along with the organized proletariat, other progressive and patriotic forces are also taking part in this struggle. The peasants, the middle strata of the population, the young generation, the students, the women and even some military are increasingly becoming involved in it. Organized industrial action has grown to an unprecedented scale.

The growing unity of the workers' movement in defence of the vital interests of the working people, against unemployment, inflation and the predatory policies of the monopolies is a factor of immense significance. The international cohesion of the working class and its organizations, reflecting the law-governed process towards internationalization of the class struggle, is growing stronger.

The period *after the Tenth Congress showed the correctness of our policy towards the industrialized capitalist states.* This is a policy aimed at consolidating the principles of peaceful coexistence, at promoting equitable and mutually advantageous cooperation. During the last few years, ten-year agreements on economic cooperation were signed with a number of advanced capitalist countries. Particularly important were the summit meetings with the leaders of the FRG, Italy, Austria, France, Sweden and some other countries. Our contacts with these countries are acquiring an increasingly businesslike and constructive character and are assisting the consolidation of détente. We welcome the willingness for cooperation displayed by a number of Western governments, political and business circles.

The Helsinki Conference opened up fresh vistas for the policy of détente and cooperation. Much still remains to be done, however, in order to achieve the full and complete implementation of the provisions and principles of the Final Act by all signatories, to supplement political with military détente, to make irreversible the process of easing international tension.

We are in favour of putting an end to the arms race, of reducing military stockpiles. We are in favour of *disarmament*. It is universally known that whatever has been accomplished, whatever is being done, has been accomplished and is being done at the initiative of the Soviet Union and the Warsaw Treaty countries. These initiatives are still open questions and the response of the capitalist states has still to come. Among them are the proposals for concluding international treaties on a general and complete ban on nuclear tests, on prohibiting and destroying chemical weapons, on banning the development of new types and systems of weapons of mass destruction as well as on the prohibition to adversely influence the natural environment by military or other hostile acts. In this respect a great role has to be played by the World Disarmament Conference which should be convened at the earliest possible date. Efforts have to be made to activate the talks on the reduction of troops and armaments in Central Europe and to adopt concrete measures in this connexion. We hope that the Western states will respond with the necessary realism to enable us at last to set out along the road to the ultimate goal: general and complete disarmament.

We fully support the proposal of the 25th Congress of the CPSU for concluding a *world treaty renouncing the use of force in international relations*. This proposal is entirely in the spirit of the peace-loving foreign policy pursued by the USSR and the other fraternal socialist states, in the spirit of Helsinki.

Our country shall work consistently to achieve the abolition of discrimination and all kinds of limitations in international trade, which should be placed on an equal and mutually advantageous footing. We expect that the constructive proposals of the Council for Mutual Economic Assistance for expanding its relations with the Common Market will be accepted and will be instrumental in developing the economic ties between the European states.

In the current climate of détente the *peoples of Asia, Africa and Latin America have achieved fresh major victories* in the struggle for national liberation, for political and economic progress. Substantial changes have taken place in the alignment of the class forces within these countries. In a number of countries, the anti-imperialist tendencies grew stronger. These countries have started building up independent national economies and establishing a progressive social structure. The popularity of socialist ideas is growing. Good prospects have emerged for further extending the struggle against the racist regimes in Africa. In the countries where a capitalist structure has already been established or is being formed now, the unity of the left and democratic forces in defence of the economic and the political interests of the working people is growing.

Progressive and revolutionary-democratic changes are meeting with fierce opposition on the part of the forces of imperialism and neocolonialism. The latter resort to various means of applying pressure, including aggressive wars and antipopular coups.

By scheming and plotting, the imperialists managed to reverse the development of Chile. But this was a Pyrrhic victory. Despite the brutal terror, the Chilean people did not fall and will never fall on its knees. Its just struggle is intensifying and will continue to intensify. Hundreds of millions óf people all over the world side with it. From the rostrum of the Congress, we voice our fraternal solidarity with the Chilean communists and socialists, with all Chilean patriots. We insist: Freedom for the repressed and martyred people of Chile! Freedom for the heroic son of the Chilean people, for our comrade and brother Luis Corvalan!

The military-fascist takeover was indeed a bitter lesson in class struggle, and the leftist and democratic forces in the capitalist and the developing countries cannot but learn from it. They will not let another Chilean tragedy happen again, they will not let their peoples, which have chosen or will choose the road of socialist development, be drowned in blood.

The imperialists and their supporters are to blame that the hotbed of war in the *Middle East* is still alive. The danger of a new conflagration in this part of the world will persist as long as the Israeli troops continue to occupy the Arab territories they seized in 1967, as long as the Arab people of Palestine is not given the possibility of having a state of its own, as long as conditions do not exist for all states and peoples in the region to live in peace and security. A just and lasting solution to the Middle East issue can only be achieved at the Geneva conference with the participation of the Organization for the Liberation of Palestine, which is the only legitimate representative of the Arab people of Palestine.

In spite of flagrant imperialist interference, the *people of Angola,* supported by the socialist states and the progressive forces throughout the world, defeated the aggressors and the forces of internal reaction and saved the People's Republic of Angola.

Historic experience proves beyond any doubt that no force can crush the will of the peoples, set on building in freedom their new life!

The further strengthening of the anti-imperialist unity of the newly liberated and developing countries, their cooperation with the socialist countries and with all progressive forces throughout the world is a guarantee of this. The experience gained so far shows unequivocally that the newly liberated states can best defend their national interests by steering a course of progressive social transformations, by waging a consistent struggle against those responsible for their backwardness.

Loyal to its international duty, socialist Bulgaria is providing selfless moral, political and material support to these countries and is expanding its cooperation with them. The relations of our Party with the governing progressive and democratic parties and the national-liberation movements have become closer and more intensive. We are maintaining close ties with the Front for the Liberation of Mozambique, with the Popular Movement for the Liberation of Angola, with the Organization for the Liberation of Palestine, and many more.

The summit talks with the leaders of India, Algeria, Mozambique, the People's Republic of Congo, the People's Democratic Republic of Yemen, Iraq, Syria, Iran, Tunisia, Mauritania, etc. contributed substantially to the strengthening of friendly relations. The People's Republic of Bulgaria shall continue to intensify its political, economic and cultural contacts with the developing countries.

Comrades,
Against the background of the general trend towards European and world political détente, our country has worked intensely and has achieved a great deal in improving its political, economic and cultural relations with its Balkan neighbours.

The Bulgarian Communist Party continues to attach special importance to our relations with the *neighbouring socialist states*. We regard these relations as a major factor in strengthening peace, security and cooperation in the Balkans.

In recent years, our all-round cooperation with the *Socialist Republic of Romania* has continued to develop and expand successfully. In the future, too, we shall promote the political, economic and cultural cooperation between our two socialist countries, we shall expand the ties between the Party, state, economic and public bodies and organizations, between the towns and the districts of the two countries.

We are pursuing a consistent policy of friendship and are developing relations with the *Socialist Federal Republic of Yugoslavia.* As a result of the efforts made, political contacts, economic cooperation and cultural links are making good headway. We attach great importance to the activation of relations between the Bulgarian Communist Party and the Union of Yugoslav Communists, and shall continue to do everything that lies in our power to promote friendship between the two countries.

During the period under review, we made steps to normalize relations with *Albania,* but these did not meet with the necessary understanding. In spite of that, we shall continue to work in the same direction, which is in the interest of the two peoples.

Our relations with *Turkey* and with *Greece* are characterized by a steady development of political contacts, of economic and cultural cooperation. With both countries we signed declarations on the principles of goodneighbourliness, which provide a firm basis for the further development of our relations.

Our stand on the *Cyprus problem* is principled and

consistent. We are for the preservation of the sovereignty, independence and territorial integrity of the Republic of Cyprus, we are against the imperialist encroachments, against foreign interference in the internal affairs of this much tried country.

While pointing to the favourable development of the relations of the People's Republic of Bulgaria with the Balkan states, we are far from idealizing the present situation in this part of Europe where various political orientations and ideological trends exist, and where the situation is still complex and controversial. Certain imperialist circles of NATO, assisted by the Maoists, do not desist from their attempts to torpedo the process of détente.

The People's Republic of Bulgaria shall in the future, too, remain loyal to its principled and constructive peaceloving Balkan policy which is not influenced by any ad hoc motives.

We shall continue to work consistently to turn the Balkans into a region of good-neighbourly relations, understanding and cooperation. Let the dark past of hostility and bloody wars between the Balkan states be confined for ever to the museum of history!

Comrades,

At the 25th Congress of the CPSU, Comrade Leonid Ilyich Brezhnev presented a *Programme which was approved by the Congress for the further struggle for peace and international cooperation,* for freedom and independence of the peoples. This programme is a natural continuation of the Peace Programme proclaimed by the 24th Congress of the CPSU. It provides fresh proof that socialism and peace are indivisible. The Soviet Union has again proved to be an invincible bulwark of peace and social progress throughout the world.

On behalf of the Bulgarian communists, on behalf of the Bulgarian working people, allow me to declare solemnly from this rostrum that *the Bulgarian Communist Party and the People's Republic of Bulgaria, all of us give our wholehearted support to this programme and adopt it as our own!* We shall do everything within our power and shall work relentlessly so that it may be implemented in real life, so that the life-giving sun of just peace, freedom, independence and cooperation among the peoples may shine ever brighter on our planet!

Comrades,

Life itself is confirming in an increasingly convincing way the paramount role of the international communist movement in accelerating world social progress. In recent years it scored fresh successes; it enhanced its role as the most influential political force of our time.

The active participation of the communists in the implementation of the anti-imperialist platform of the 1969 Moscow Conference has proved extremely fruitful. The support given to the Vietnamese people, to the Arab peoples, to our Chilean brothers in class, to the communists and the other democratic forces in the capitalist countries, as well as a number of other manifestations of unity and solidarity have confirmed *the immense strength of the unity of the communist parties.*

Bilateral and multilateral cooperation between the fraternal parties has expanded. New types of links and exchange of experience have been introduced and found productive. It goes without saying that differences due to the complexity of the setup, to the variety of problems and the conditions in which they are being solved, may and in fact do arise. It is important, however, that such problems should be solved in a comradely way, in the spirit of the principles of Marxism-Leninism and proletarian internationalism, that the fraternal parties should join efforts in outlining the ways leading to the common communist goals and ideals. In this way the ranks and the positions of the fraternal parties will grow stronger and our international unity will be reinforced.

Every fraternal party, in keeping with the specific conditions, elaborates individually its strategic and tactical policy for reaching the goals of the revolution on a national scale. At the same time, under the present setup the internationalist responsibility of every party to the common communist cause is growing. *The guarantee for the success of every communist party and of the international communist movement as a whole lies in our unity, created and steeled in decade-long class struggles.*

It is worth mentioning that during the period following the Tenth Congress the international activity of the Bulgarian Communist Party grew and became enriched and its efficiency increased. 566 delegations and working groups from a large number of parties were received in this country, and 334 Bulgarian delegations and working groups visited other countries. In 1975 and the first three months of 1976 our country was visited by 26 presidents, general or first secretaries of fraternal parties.

The Bulgarian Communist Party will continue to make its specific contribution to the various initiatives

46

of the communist movement. Attaching great significance to the conference of the European communist and workers' parties, the Bulgarian Communist Party is participating most actively in its preparation. In the interest of the struggle for the unity of the working class, for peace, security, democracy and social progress, our Party will expand the contacts and cooperation with the socialist and social-democratic parties. At the same time it will continue to oppose social-reformism as an ideology alien to Marxism-Leninism.

The true interests of the communist parties, of the working class and of all working people, of the entire *anti-imperidlist front require that the struggle against right and 'left' revisionism, against nationalism and anti-Sovietism should continue.* The degradation of Maoism has reached a new phase. It entered into an alliance with the most aggressive forces of imperialism, fascism and revanchism, with the opponents of peaceful coexistence and social progress. Its actions are becoming ever more dangerous to peace and the security of the peoples. The policy and ideology of the present Chinese leadership are deeply hostile to Marxism-Leninism, to the communist ideal. Our Party considers it its duty to participate unreservedly in the struggle against Maoism, for its total political and ideological defeat.

Profound changes have occurred in recent years in the international situation. New, extremely important tasks are now facing the communist movement. For that reason, the Bulgarian Communist Party is of the opinion that conditions are at hand *to prepare and hold a new world conference of the communist and workers' parties.*

The Party of the Bulgarian communists, true to its

47

revolutionary traditions, will continue to contribute to the collective discussion and solution of the problems currently facing the modern world and the world revolutionary process, for strengthening and consolidating the sacred communist fraternity!

Such is, Comrades, the situation in the world. Such are the principal trends of our future work on the international arena. In carrying it out we draw and will continue to draw strength from the unshakable conviction that the foreign policy of the Bulgarian Communist Party corresponds to the interests and aspirations of our peace-loving and heroic people and relies on its unconditional support. We draw strength from the unshakable conviction that this policy is correct, that it is in full conformity with the objective tendencies of development in the world and in the world revolutionary process. It corresponds to the vital interests of the world socialist community and the international communist movement, the interests of all peoples fighting for freedom and independence, for peace and social progress.

II. THE POLICY AND TASKS OF THE PARTY IN THE SPHERE OF ECONOMY AND SCIENTIFIC AND TECHNOLOGICAL PROGRESS

Comrades,

The review of what has been achieved since the Tenth Congress in the sphere of economy and of scientific and technological progress proves that, under the leadership of the Bulgarian Communist Party, our people has conquered new summits in building a developed socialist society. The country's economic potential and defence capability have increased significantly. The contribution of science and education to the material and cultural progress of our country has grown, too.

1. MAIN RESULTS OF THE IMPLEMENTATION OF THE SIXTH FIVE-YEAR PLAN IN THE ECONOMIC SPHERE

What were, during the Sixth Five-year Plan, the most salient features of the development of the economy, the sphere which determines our overall social development?

The construction and consolidation of the material and technical base of socialism continued at an accelerated rate during the five years between the Tenth and the Eleventh Party Congresses. Capital investments during this period totalled 21,000 million leva. At the end of 1975 fixed capital came up to over 32,000 million leva. The task of steadily raising the country's industrial level and of putting all economic sectors on an industrial basis is being successfully translated into reality.

The economy developed dynamically, with Bulgaria holding one of the leading places in the world in terms of growth rate. The national income has risen by 46 per cent. Labour productivity has increased by over 44 per cent. Higher labour productivity accounted for as much as 98.6 per cent of the national income accretion.

Qualitative changes have occurred in the structure of production. The ratio between industrial and agricultural production has changed from 77.1:22.9 to 81.2:18.8. The relative share of industry in the national income went up from 49 per cent in 1970 to 54.6 per cent in 1975. Production in industries on which technological progress and the effectivity of the national economy depend most, has been developing at priority rates. Among them are the power industry, including nuclear power industry, the chemical and petrochemical industries, mechanical engineering and especially electronics. Light and food industry production has also been boosted. The variety of consumer goods has increased and their quality improved.

Despite unfavourable climatic conditions, agriculture has scored major successes. The volume of agricultural production has been increasing by an annual average of 3.1 per cent. Grain production has registered the most rapid growth. Meat, milk and egg production has increased considerably.

The other economic sectors have also been developing at high rates.

The intensification of the national economy through concentration and specialization of production and through the reconstruction and modernization of production capacities has continued over the past five years. New equipment and advanced technological methods have been introduced in the key branches of material production. The activities of the Party in the sphere of scientific and technological progress to which it attaches prime importance, have been aimed at fulfilling the task of linking up the scientific and technological revolution with the advantages of the socialist social system and of ensuring creative unity between science and production, between science and social development.

The National Party Conference has given a powerful impetus to the efforts of the Party and economic bodies and organizations and the workforce to achieve *a rapid rise in labour productivity,* more rational utilization of production capacities and economical use of raw materials, fuel and energy.

Noting the achievements during the period under review, the Party's Central Committee has not remained blind to the shortcomings and problems still outstanding in the economic sphere. It should be openly said that the plan was not fulfilled according to some indices. Full-capacity operation in some already commissioned capacities of the engineering and the chemical industries and other branches has been delayed. A number of projects were not completed within the set terms. Production facilities have been allowed to stay idle or to work at less than full capacity. In some branches the task of introducing new machines and advanced technological methods has not been fulfilled. In general, the tardy application of scientific results in practice and the insufficient utilization of foreign scientific and technological achievements is one of our serious shortcomings. Nor can we be satisfied with the rate at which reconstruction and modernization have been carried out. Violation of labour and technological discipline and considerable losses of working time are tolerated in some places.

The shortcomings and difficulties in the economy are primarily of a subjective nature: they are mainly due to mistakes and still persisting weaknesses in economic management on the part of the respective economic, state and Party bodies and organizations. The overcoming of these weaknesses is essential for the further successful development of our economy.

2. THE SEVENTH FIVE-YEAR PLAN – A PERIOD OF INCREASED EFFECTIVITY AND HIGH QUALITY

Comrades,
The Party's Central Committee submits for discussion and approval by the Eleventh Party Congress Guidelines for the Socio-economic Development of the People's Republic of Bulgaria during the Seventh Five-year Plan. This document reflects the substance of our policy towards the realization of the immediate historic

task of the Party, namely, the building of a developed socialist society. It was published and discussed extensively at district Party conferences, Party meetings, meetings of the working people and in the press. Everywhere it brought a broad response and won full approval; useful considerations and practical suggestions were put forward. It is proper that these numerous suggestions be carefully examined and the most expedient of them be taken into consideration in working out the Seventh Five-year Plan.

The principal socio-economic task of the Seventh Five-year Plan is to pursue unswervingly the Party policy of fuller satisfaction of the material and cultural needs of the population by ensuring a dynamic and proportional development of the national economy, by rapidly raising labour productivity, efficiency and quality by means of modernization, reconstruction, concentration and accelerated introduction of the scientific and technological achievements and by raising the socialist consciousness of the working people and establishing the socialist lifestyle. This task is to be carried out under the conditions of deepening socialist integration.

The strategic line of the Party's economic policy of further intensification of production, and a decisive rise in the effectivity of the economy and the quality of production substantially enhances *the role and responsibility of our scientists*. It calls for linking most closely the advancement of the scientific front and scientific research in the social, natural and technical sciences with the main trends and concrete needs of material production and our entire socio-economic development. Fundamental and applied research, especially in the natural and mathematical sciences, should be steered to goal-specific problems related to the expansion of the country's raw material and energy resources, the utilization of the achievements of the chemistry of high polymers and the extensive use of chemicals in the economy, the raising of biological productivity, the development of biologically active substances and biological products which can be applied in industry, agriculture and medicine, the evolvement of more effective technologies and the production of better-quality goods.

The rapid and effective introduction of the achievements of science and technology in production acquires prime significance. It should be regarded as an exceptionally important link in the research-production chain. In conjunction with this, it is urgently necessary to improve the mechanism of planning and incentives so as to step up decisively the introduction of the achievements of science and technology and to make enterprises emulate in introducing novelties. In addition to our own achievements, we must do our utmost to make use of the results of world science and technology as a key factor in raising the technical and technological level of production. The development and intensification of scientific research and pilot work with the fraternal socialist countries and, in the first place, with the Soviet Union, the all-round rapprochement with the USSR in the field of science and technological progress is a key trend in our scientific and technological policy. This enables us to save time, efforts and money, to use most rationally and effectively the scientific potential.

In the coming period, we are to embark on a course

54

of *transition from an extensive to a predominantly intensive development of scientific activity and a decisive rise in its effectivity.* Already during the Seventh Five-year Plan, the economic effect of applied research and development is to rise between four and five times over the present level. The intensification of scientific work calls for providing wider opportunities for the energy, abilities and talent of the scientists, for using the still unexplored possibilities of the scientific potential, and for achieving a considerable improvement in the material and technical base of science. The question of cadres and their qualitative composition is the pivotal problem of the intensification of the scientific front. This requires substantial improvements in the system of selection and development of scientific cadres and higher standards when awarding scientific degrees and titles. The training of young specialists worthy of the noble mission of scientists should be the object of particular concern. This in turn calls for keeping university training abreast of the front ranks of science and its latest trends.

Besides the improvement of the qualitative composition of the scientific cadre, the improvement of the living and working conditions of scientists and the further raising of their public prestige is a matter of particular importance. The specific nature of scientific work requires that special attention be paid to the correct regulation of social relationships in science and to the establishment of a creative atmosphere in the scientific teams. We attach paramount importance to the unfolding of creative discussions, criticism and the clash of opinion as a way to the progress of science and a means of overcoming monopolism in it.

The role of the *Bulgarian Academy of Sciences* is enhanced still higher in the light of the qualitatively new tasks facing the scientific front. The Party appreciates highly its activities which have become increasingly linked to the needs of production and social practice in recent years. We shall continue to work to develop the Bulgarian Academy of Sciences as a leading scientific organization called upon to make a substantial contribution to the advancement of Bulgarian science and culture, to accelerate scientific and technological progress and lend assistance in the rational utilization of the achievements of science and technology.

Still wider vistas for action are being opened up before *the movement of innovators and inventors* to which goes much of the credit for raising the technical standards of production. Also on the increase is the role of *the scientific and technical unions* which should be a broad public base of the efforts for a speedier and more effective application of technical and technological achievements in practice and for the dissemination of scientific and technical knowledge.

The Committee for Science, Technological Progress and Higher Education did fruitful work for promoting scientific and technological progress and the training of highly qualified cadres. It is necessary to further increase the exigence and enhance the role of the Committee *as a new state-cum-public body,* which is invested with the main responsibility of carrying out our unified national scientific and technological policy in all spheres of public activity. This calls for an enhancement of the role and responsibility of Ministries and departments in accelerating scientific and technological progress and the more rapid introduction in practice of scientific and technological achievements.

The principal ways of speeding up technological progress during the Seventh Five-year Plan should be the introduction of entirely new technological methods and machines in the key production branches, mechanization of auxiliary processes, mechanization and automation in production, as well as automatic control of both individual technological processes and whole manufacturing systems. Expedient efforts are needed *to turn the seventh five-year period into a period of gradual transition from manufacturing systems involving single machines and technological processes to manufacturing systems employing on a mass scale highly effective systems of machines, equipment, devices and technological methods which ensure complete mechanization and automation of the production processes.* Moreover, it should be borne in mind that the achievements of scientific and technological progress can only be used extensively and effectively in the conditions of a further concentration and specialization of the economy on a nationwide scale, through the development of standardization, unification and typification of items, parts, assemblies and processes, and through optimal specialization of enterprises and economic units.

Scientific and technological progress is not an end in itself. It should lead to savings of raw and prime materials, energy and labour, to higher labour productivity, lower production costs, better quality of goods and, ultimately, to general rise in the effectivity of the whole national economy.

Allow me to dwell in brief on some of these questions.

The first of them concerns the concentration, specialization and updating of production within the framework of the whole national economy.

An improvement in the approach to concentration, specialization and updating of production is necessary at the present stage. What we need now is not merely concentration, specialization, updating and reconstruction within individual production and economic units, ministries and departments, but large-scale changes in the organization of production and the production links on a national scale. The concentration and specialization of production should develop on a much broader basis so as to encompass the technologically specialized manufacturing systems, irrespective of their organizational subordination — from the designing of their products, the production of raw materials, billets, parts and pre-fabs to the assembly, ˙packing and marketing of the goods, as well as their maintenance and repair during exploitation.

A key element here is the large-scale standardization, unification and typification of the manufactured parts, assemblies and items and the creation of optimal capacities with a view to meeting the needs of the whole national economy. This calls for the creation and introduction already during the Seventh Five-year Plan of uniform national systems of catalogues of standardized parts, assemblies and items for the different branches. The catalogues will have the force of laws which will regulate production relationships.

The Party's Central Committee believes that *the improvement in the approach to the concentration, specialization and updating of production is of key importance for our economy and for raising its effectivity.* That is why it has set the task to concretize the approach and apply it in transport engineering, construction, the light and furniture-making industry, the national transport complex and other branches, and has adopted a line of consistently applying it in all economic sectors in which this is possible. The work done to date by many workforces of engineers, economists, mathematicians, cybernetics experts and other specialists from the respective branches gives us reason to claim that this will ensure the further acceleration of the development of the productive forces and will make it possible to orientate capital investment correctly and utilize it most rationally.

The specialization of whole chains of enterprises in initial raw material processing, the production of prime materials and the manufacture of parts, assemblies and finished products, as well as the construction of production and assembly enterprises of optimal capacity will make it possible to adapt quickly to the requirements of the international and home market and to spot in time the bottlenecks in the development of the various branches. This will also pave the way for more effective scientific back-up services for production, a wider use of advanced technologies and the quota-based system of planning, accounting, incentives and responsibility, for a more rational utilization of the fixed capital, for greater savings of labour and materials and for a substantial rise in the effectivity of production. In view of all this, the updating and reconstruction of the economic sectors and the distribution of capital investment, of material and manpower resources during the Seventh Five-year Plan should be effected on this basis.

An untapped reserve in raising the effectivity of the national economy in the conditions of deepening concentration and specialization is *the proper territorial distribution of the separate branches, subbranches and manufacturing systems.* It can be said that we have so far failed to use rationally the enormous possibilities which a better territorial structure of production offers. That is why during the Seventh Five-year Plan period specialization in the manufacture of parts, assemblies and items and technological specialization should go hand in hand with territorial concentration and specialization.

The second problem concerns the necessity of a campaign for saving on labour, raw and prime materials and energy. For us, this problem will continue to grow in importance and complexity, due especially to the increasing shortage of manpower and the inadequate natural resources of the country.

According to demographic forecasts, there will be no significant change in the size of the working population in this country in the next five years. At the same time, the number of those engaged in the sphere of communal services will rise. Consequently, we can expect a certain drop in the number of people engaged in the sphere of material production.

Obviously, the fact is not without importance that the economical and effective use of the labour force, of raw and prime materials, of fuel and energy is a decisive factor in reducing production costs and in raising the profitability of production.

Because of all this, *reduced consumption of labour and materials in production and the rational use of labour resources must become one of the keys to achieving the further speedy and effective development of the economy.*

The efforts aimed at solving this problem must concentrate, firstly on reducing the consumption of labour, raw and prime materials and energy per unit of production through changes in designing, technology, etc., and, secondly, towards improving the structure of production through a decreased relative share of labour- and material-intensive production. In per-unit consumption of labour, raw and prime materials during the Seventh Five-year Plan we shall have to reach the level of the most advanced countries in this sphere.

The third problem concerns the necessity for a decisive rise in the quality of production. We have dwelt on this problem in detail on a number of occasions in the past. I am sure you will agree that there is no further need to point out either its economic, political or ideological importance. What is needed is action, action and more action! The attainment of high quality of production is, and must remain, a foremost task for the Party and the state, for the leading cadres, for the specialist-constructors, technologists, designers, the workers and farmers. The execution of this task must be tackled in its complexity, encompassing all quality-forming elements, all technological stages at which quality is being created, all links, means and conditions that form part of this comprehensive process. Concern for quality should begin at the research institutes, it should be a key problem in designing and standardization, in production and quality control, and it should end with the packaging, transportation, storage and consumption of production. The final results will be good only if this 'quality chain' functions flawlessly.

Especially important in this respect is the improvement of the system of incentives, coupled with stern measures against those who have an irresponsible and even criminal attitude to matters relating to quality. Our prime economic and patriotic task is to raise to new heights of excellence the trade-mark of Bulgarian production.

The fourth problem concerns the fuller satisfaction of the economy's needs for highly-qualified cadres.

We consider the education and qualification of the cadres, and especially of the younger generation, an activity of strategic importance. That is why, during the period under review, the Central Committee continued to pay special attention to education, to making it correspond to the present-day needs of society. Some 305,000 skilled workers, 195,000 secondary school and college students and over 70,000 university students were trained during the past five years, making a sum-total of over 570,000 qualified cadres, as compared to the 410,305 who received their training under the Fifth Five-year Plan.

Nowadays even greater demands are being made on people's general educational and specialized training. This makes it necessary to complete in general outline our transition to general secondary education during the Seventh Five-year Plan. On the other hand, the system of general education will have to be reorganized so as to incorporate material production as one of its component parts. After a certain period of study at the unified polytechnical schools, the students will have to be included in material production, on which basis they should continue their education and all-round development, gaining at one and the same time a qualification, fulfilment and adaptability through their work. In this way *production and the workforce become a laboratory for the intellectual, occupational, moral and aesthetic development of the individual, a principal basis for the control and self-assertion through labour of each and every student*. This change should, of course, be approached carefully and gradually, after successful experimentation. This enhances significantly the role and responsibility of the *Ministry of Education*. It should be borne in mind that the introduction of students over a certain age to material production does not, by any means, imply a rejection or even a slight underestimation of the efforts for further solid acquiring of scientific knowledge. What is needed is even greater care for the communist upbringing of the students, for their growing up into ideologically convinced builders of socialism.

The role of the teachers will continue to grow. To them, to these selfless moulders of the all-round personalities of the students, go our sincerest and most profound acknowledgements from his rostrum.

Our Party will continue to promote the development of *higher education*, for achieving a decisive rise in the level of qualification of our young specialists. A basic guideline for the improvement of the training of university students should be its direct linking with material production and social practice. On the other hand, we must no longer put up with the unsatisfactory instruction in ideological subjects. Decisive measures are needed in this respect.

At the present stage education ceases to be a one-time process. The rapid development of science and technology, the appearance of new spheres of production, raises acutely the problem of *organizing a comprehensive system for the specialization, re-training and requalification of the specialists and workforces*. The task of ensuring additional training and post-graduate qualification in the new, promising branches of science and technology, in the guidance of the scientific and technological process, in its introduction into practice, etc., has become yet more pressing. More specifically, measures should be taken for improving the education of workers and cooperative farmers under the age of 40 through evening and correspondence courses and in the workers' classes at the secondary schools. Special care should be taken for raising the skills of working mothers in industry and agriculture.

The Central Committee is profoundly convinced that the many-thousand-strong army of teachers and lecturers, scientists and technological experts will make their worthy contribution to the country's scientific and technological progress, to the upbringing of an educated, physically and ideologically sound young generation, a generation ready to work and fight in the name of our great cause!

Comrades,

The solving of these basic problems of our economy, the fulfilment of the decisions of the present Eleventh

Party Congress will give fresh impetus to the development of the country's productive forces and to the intensification of the national economy, will speed up scientific and technological progress and lead to the raising of labour productivity. And we are fully justified in maintaining that *the Seventh Five-year Plan will be a five-year period of high effectivity and high quality.*

High effectivity and high equality – this must not be mere sloganeering, an empty phrase, it must become a fundamental mobilizing task, a goal for whose attainment all forces, knowledge and creativity of the workers, peasants and the people's intelligentsia, of all Party, public, state and economic administrative bodies and organizations must be mobilized.

3. GUIDELINES FOR THE DEVELOPMENT OF THE ECONOMIC SECTORS

What are the guidelines for the development of the different sectors of the economy during the Seventh Five-year Plan?

During the Seventh Five-year Plan, as well as up to 1990, *industrial production* will grow at a rapid pace. At the same time the development of the heavy industry and of the industries producing consumer goods will also be speeded up. We must ensure that the production of consumer goods grows faster than do the population's earnings.

Naturally, this does not reverse our general policy of striving for the rapid development of the production of means of production. On the contrary, all branches of the heavy industry will continue to develop at high growth rates. Special attention must be paid to solving three key problems:

first, the problem of energy and raw materials;

second, the accelerated development and the structural improvement of machine-building, including the development of fixed capital machine-building.

third, the dynamic development of the chemical industry.

The national economy's growing needs for *energy* will be satisfied through better exploitation of existing capacities, through the accelerated development of nuclear power production, through the use of other energy sources and through wider participation in the unified energy system of the socialist states, members of the Council for Mutual Economic Assistance. This will allow us to ensure the necessary reserves of power-generating capacities. By 1980 annual power generation will reach nearly 38,000 million kWh, 20 per cent of which will be produced by nuclear power stations.

The prospecting for *raw materials,* especially for ores of ferrous, non-ferrous, rare and precious metals, for oil, natural gas and mineral deposits must continue unabated. Parallel with the expanded exploitation of local raw material resources, the comprehensive evaluation of our mineral resources, their classification and standardization, as well as their most effective use both according to type and to the order of extraction, will continue to grow in importance. In the construction of extraction capacities, attention should be focussed on creating optimal enterprises using the most effective technologies aimed at the complex exploitation of all useful component parts.

There is also a very large and untapped source in the creation of a modern system for the collection and processing of the growing quantities of *utility scrap*, and in its use we must catch up with the advanced industrial countries.

The role of *ferrous metals* in the all-round development of the economy in the coming years will continue to grow. That is why we are faced with the task of reconstructing, updating and expanding the existing production capacities and of ensuring that they work at full capacity. By 1980 the annual production of ferrous metals must reach nearly four million tons.

The construction and commissioning of new mining capacities is envisaged in the field of *non-ferrous metallurgy*, as well as the updating and reconstruction and the introduction of advanced technologies in the existing capacities, with the aim of ensuring raw materials for the necessary growth in the production of copper, lead, zinc and other non-ferrous metals.

Machine-building, being the core of the country's industrialization, must continue its dynamic development during the Seventh Five-year Plan, in order to ensure a better supply of machines and fixed capital equipment to the key branches of the economy. The volume of its production is nearly to double. Efforts must be directed towards the setting up of auxiliary facilities, with the aim of overcoming the existing disproportion between the castings, calkings, ganging materials, of other elements, units and parts and the assembly capacities.

Machine-building is faced with the task of speedily

starting the production of automatic machines and units, assembly lines and systems, and complete plant, as well as the production of computing machinery which Bulgaria specializes in. During the current five-year plan, the country must also begin to specialize in the production of complete plant for the power-generation, mining, chemical and food industries.

The production structure of transport equipment, farm machinery, shipbuilding, of machine tools, and electrical and electronic engineering should also be improved.

The guidelines for the development of *the chemical industry* envisage the expansion of the range of chemical products and the launching of the production of new, promising chemical products, with special emphasis being laid on the various types of polymers: plastics, synthetic fibres and synthetic rubber. Also envisaged is the further development of the petrochemical industry, the production of fertilizers, industrial microbiology, the pharmaceutical industry, perfumery and cosmetics, the cellulose and paper industry, and small-tonnage chemistry. For this purpose, the guidelines call for the construction of new production capacities equipped with the most up-to-date technology.

Despite the significant growth in *the production of manufactured consumer goods* during the last five years, this is still lagging behind the growing needs of the population. We must take into account the fact that the demand for such goods will increase during the Seventh Five-year Plan.

This faces our light industry with the serious task of producing larger quantities and a greater variety of better-quality goods for all age groups of the population.

Is the industry ready to meet this objective demand? Our light industry has considerable capacities. What is more, it will benefit from significant capital investments in the next few years.

What is needed here?

The industry should show flexibility in adapting to the rapidly changing demand and the rising incomes of the population, it should take greater note of the tastes and preferences of consumers, should conform more fully to the sound trends in fashion, and so on.

Manufactured consumer goods should be of high quality and should be constantly brought up to date. Let us ensure that many of our consumer goods compare favourably with the best in the world!

Further on, a common practice should be put a stop to, namely, that of limiting or completely terminating the production of goods that are essential, cheap and in great demand under the pretext of replacing 'outdated' goods with new products.

During the Seventh Five-year Plan there must be a significant rise in the production of textiles, ready-to-wear clothes, shoes, knitwear and children's goods, paralleled by the very nearly full satisfaction of the demand for consumer durables such as furniture, radio and television sets, refrigerators, washing machines and the like. In keeping with this, light industry production is envisaged to grow by about 45 per cent as against 1975.

During the same period *food industry* production will increase by about 40 per cent. There will be a sharp increase in the production of processed, ready-to-cook and ready-to-serve foods.

We are confident that the workers, the scientific and technological and all administrative cadres working in industry will readily respond to the Party's call for better and more effective work, for increasing their contribution to the development of the economic potential of our socialist homeland!

Comrades,

Agriculture will always play an exceptionally important role in the development of the national economy and in improving the well-being of the people. That is why the Party will continue to pay very great attention to this sector of the economy. Agriculture will receive more funds and material resources during the Seventh Five-year Plan than in the past five years.

At its plenary session in November 1973, the Party's Central Committee drew up a long-term comprehensive programme for raising agricultural standards. The fulfilment of this programme during the Seventh Five-year Plan will create conditions for decisively improving the population's food supplies, as well as industry's supply with raw materials of agricultural origin. The necessary conditions are at hand for increasing agricultural production by about 20 per cent over the five-year period.

As in the past, the expansion of grain production remains a key task, on the basis of which the *fodder problem* must be solved. Our country has big reserves for stepping up fodder production, including the production of grain fodder. These reserves are connected with the better and scientifically-based regionalization of grain crops ; with the introduction of high-yielding varieties and hybrids; with the use of totally new technologies or new technological elements in grain production; with the introduction of systems of machines for the complex mechanization of farming from soil preparation to the timely and complete harvesting, storing and processing of the crops.

Special attention must be paid to the full use of rough fodder, which continues to be wasted or burned. Studies indicate that over 50 per cent of the leafage and stalks of the grain crops remain unutilized. New technologies for making wholesome fodder out of the leafage, stalks and roots of grain and other crops should be developed with the aim of achieving their maximum assimilation by the ruminants, and, whenever possible, by the non-ruminants as well.

During the current five-year period we must do away with the underrating of the *soya bean* as a fundamental protein fodder crop.

The transition to a unified balance of grain fodder for the whole country will have a positive effect on making the most rational use of our fodder resources.

The Party's Central Committee considers the significant growth of *livestock production* a foremost task, for whose fulfilment our agriculture must mobilize its full potential. The necessary conditions are at hand for placing to a large extent our cooperative and state stock-breeding on an industrial basis during the Seventh Five-year Plan through the use of the most effective and progressive solutions. Pedigree stock, especially in cattle-raising, play an important role in the advance of stockbreeding. And if this problem has to a certain extent been solved in poultry-breeding and pig-raising, it still remains open in cattle- and sheep-raising.

Work to develop stockbreeding in the mountainous and hilly regions should be consistently expanded. On no account must stockbreeding within the framework of *personal farms* be underrated. Measures should be taken to encourage its further development as a reserve in increasing livestock production.

Along with the development of grain production and stockbreeding, the increase in the output of fruits, vegetables, grapes, tobacco and sugar beet under the Seventh Five-year Plan will be of great importance for the national economy.

In the period between the Tenth and the Eleventh Congresses, *the agro-industrial complexes*, as a higher form of economic and social organization in rural life, continued to be consolidated and further improved. They have passed the test of time with flying colours. The agro-industrial complexes which created favourable conditions for the concentration of agricultural production and putting it on an industrial basis have made a major contribution to the increase of farm produce and to gradually bridging the gap between town and village. The task now is ever more fully to tap and utilize the advantages of the agro-industrial and industrial-agrarian complexes.

The Seventh Five-year Plan will see the continuation of the process of concentration of agricultural production on the basis of its specialization and vertical integration with the food and beverages industry, and also of the process of integration of agricultural science with production. These processes will run parallel to the extensive introduction of industrial methods in agricultural production. An organic merger of agriculture with industry will gradually take place in future.

The workers in our socialist rural economy have always set an example of self-denial and conscientiousness. There is no doubt that now, too, they will fulfil with honour the new tasks of the further progress of the rural economy!

Comrades,

An essential element of our economic policy is the further improvement of *capital construction*. The main task in that field is to raise effectiveness through concentration of capital investments, reducing the proportion of incomplete construction, through high-quality workmanship and the commissioning of the projects according to schedule. During the Seventh Five-year Plan, capital investments will increase to 30,000 million leva, of which 20,000 million leva will go for material production.

The policy of channelling capital investments chiefly for updating, overhauling and extending the existing capacities makes higher demands on the organization and management of capital construction. The overall organization of capital construction should be based on the principle of *paying for a finished construction project, completed to high standards and put into operation within the normative terms.*

It is necessary to step up the modernization of the

building materials industry, to give the go-ahead for industrial methods and technologies, to introduce new and effective building materials and to further improve the process of standardization, unification and typification of construction.

The importance of the *unified transport system* will grow steadily during the Seventh Five-year Plan period. A proportionate development of the individual types of transport will be ensured and the quality of transport services will be considerably improved by means of reconstruction, modernization and increase of capacities. Transport between the settlements within a system of settlements should be developed on the principles of urban transport. The effectiveness of the railways will be raised and the length of double-track railway lines will increase considerably, as will the total number of buses and other modern transport vehicles; the complex mechanization of loading and unloading operations will become more widespread. By 1980 freight transport will grow by about 40 per cent and passenger transport, by about 25 per cent.

In order to ensure high quality communications in the national economy and the rationalization of management processes, it is necessary to raise the technical level and thoroughly improve the functioning of the *the system of communications and information.*

Transport and communications — these are the arteries of the economy and the social organism. The Party expects of all workers in the system of transport and communications high socialist consciousness, iron discipline and impeccable work!

We should like to stress once again that the development of the various branches and of the economy as a whole will be accompanied by a further expansion and deepening of specialization and cooperation of production within the framework of the Council for Mutual Economic Assistance.

Comrades, such are the main results of the fulfilment of the Sixth Five-year Plan, and such are the basic trends in the development of our socialist economy in the coming period.

The new tasks call for even more energetic and purposeful activity on the part of the Party, state and economic bodies, the leading cadres and workers. It is necessary to further improve the system of planning and economic management, to enhance the role of financing and crediting, to increase their influence on the intensification of the national economy, the concentration and specialization of production, the reconstruction and updating of capacities, and for a decisive rise in the effectiveness and quality of economic activity.

Allow me, on behalf of the Congress, to express profound confidence that our working people, the people who have performed great feats for the upsurge of our country, will fulfil and overfulfil with honour the tasks for the development of the national economy set by the Eleventh Party Congress, and will make the Seventh Five-year Plan period an important stage in the building of a developed socialist society.

III. QUESTIONS OF THE DEVELOPMENT OF THE SOCIALIST LIFESTYLE

Comrades,

The victory of the socialist system in our country created conditions for shaping and further consolidating the socialist lifestyle.

At all stages in the development of society, the lifestyle is determined by the mode of production, by the character of the socio-economic formation. In their remarkable work *The German Ideology*, Karl Marx and Friedrich Engels stressed that the mode of production should not be seen as a mere reproduction of the people's physical existence. 'This is rather a definite mode of activity of given individuals, a definite image of their life activity, their specific *lifestyle*. The life activity of the individuals tells us what they themselves are like'. (K. Marx and F. Engels, Works, Vol. 3, p. 21, Bulgarian edition).

Life activity, as is known, embraces all spheres of human life. It includes, above all, work as a result of which material and cultural values are produced; activity through which people take part in socio-political life; activity which is the realization of the humane relationships between them, etc. The character of these activities depends on the level of the productive forces and the dominant production relations. Just as socialism is a qualitatively different, higher and more progressive social system than capitalism, *so too the socialist lifestyle is different in principle, immeasurably richer and more humane than lifestyle in a capitalist society.*

The socialist lifestyle is connected with profound changes in all spheres of human activity. Exploitation of man by man, the unjust distribution of material and cultural wealth, anti-humane relationships are done away with. Conditions are created for steadily improving the material well-being and raising the cultural standards of the population. Even when it triumphs in underdeveloped countries, socialism ensures better satisfaction of such vitally important needs of the working people as full employment, labour safety, organized holidays, child care, health services, social security and protection of motherhood than can be ensured in even the most advanced capitalist countries. Socialism guarantees free access to all types of education, creates unprecedented opportunities for familiarizing people with national and world cultural values, for the participation of the working people in socio-political life.

Social optimism, faith in the future, confidence in the morrow are among the most precious gains of the socialist worker and a distinctive feature of his life.

A vivid manifestation of the Party policy of further establishing the socialist lifestyle, of the Party's concern for man is the Programme on Raising the Standard of Living of the People, adopted at the December Plenary Session (1972).

The December Plenary Session of the Central Committee approved the attainment of a definite degree of satisfying the material and cultural needs of the people as *the foremost and immediate task of social production,* a starting point in drafting the plans for the country's socio-economic development. The Plenary Session gave a new formulation of the *scope* of the standard of living and the *manner* in which to raise it, and set the task of ensuring such a *complex* satisfaction of the material and cultural needs of the working people as corresponds to the *science-based norms of consumption* and in addition stimulates the *all-round development of the socialist personality,* and gives full play to everything that is positive and valuable in the individual.

1. MATERIAL WELL-BEING

We feel gratified to report the fact that *the Party and the people are coping successfully with the great and complex task of combining the accelerated development of the economy with the steady improvement of the people's well-being.*

During the Sixth Five-year Plan, the working people's real incomes rose by 32.4 per cent as against the 25 to 30 per cent planned in the Directives. The minimum wages went up from 65 leva in 1970 to 80 leva as early as 1973, as against the 70 leva planned in the Directives for the end of the five-year period. The average monthly nominal wages rose from 124 leva to 146 leva. The nominal incomes of the cooperative farmers almost came up to the level of those of industrial and office workers.

The objective economic laws of socialism and the fundamental interests of the people and of socialist construction demand that the paying of wages according to the quantity and quality of work done should become the basic form and source of increasing the incomes of the working people in the seventh five-year period. Therefore it is envisaged that in 1980 the average monthly nominal wages will amount to 170 leva and the minimum wages to 90 leva. The stimulating role of the *basic wages* will be enhanced. In this connection the Central Committee and the Government took a decision to carry out, during the first two years of the five-year period, a scientifically consistent reform of the wage rates.

The public consumption funds will continue to play an important role in the development of education, the health services, culture and social security during the Seventh Five-year Plan as well. They will be instrumental in putting into effect a number of social measures aimed at providing an incentive for better work to industrial and office workers and farmers, at improving the living conditions of families with many children and low incomes, of women employed in production, of pensioners, of old people who have no relatives and of students.

During the period under review, the growing demand for goods and services was more fully met.

In 1975, as compared with 1970, *per capita consumption grew as follows:* of meat and meat products – from 41.4 kg to 57 kg, of milk and dairy products – from 152.1 litres to 174 litres, of vegetables and canned vegetables – from 88.9 kg to 94 kg, of eggs – from 122 to 145. The sales of textiles, clothes, footwear and durables rose. Notwithstanding these successes the range and quality of some goods do not fully correspond to the rising purchasing power of the working people, to their more sophisticated tastes and demands, supplies of some staple goods are not regular.

During the seventh five-year period, the overall consumption of goods should rise by about 50 per cent. The growth of commodity stocks should outstrip the rise in the population's purchasing power and this should occur in a differentiated manner, taking demand into account. The most rapid growth will be in the share of durable goods and services which meet aesthetic, moral, intellectual and other spiritual needs. Opportunities will be more fully tapped for expanding trade with the Soviet Union and the other CMEA member-countries and for increasing the imports of some goods from other countries.

The raising of the standard of living and the solution of a great number of complex social problems depend to a very large extent on the smooth functioning of the service sector. It is necessary to ensure during the next five years the accelerated building of the greater part of the facilities of *the unified system for complex services in conformity with the national programme which has been worked out.*

Serious efforts will be made to improve *trade.* A system of market research and of influencing production and consumption will be created, the material and technical facilities of trade will be extended and updated. *Public catering* should ensure to the highest possible degree a rational diet for our people.

There is a considerable lag in *communal services.* During the Seventh Five-year Plan they should develop along industrial lines as a highly concentrated and modernized social production. Along with that, communal services rendered by the agro-industrial and industrial-agrarian complexes, the Central Cooperative Union and the economic organizations will expand.

The standard of trade and communal services depends to a large extent on *the work of the personnel employed in them*. Therefore, it is imperative to improve their selection and training, to adopt rates of remuneration and incentives which take into account not only the volume of trade turnover, etc., but also the number of customers who were served and the quality of the service.

The successes of our *public health services* are indisputable. From now on prophylaxis should develop further, the quality of diagnostic work and rehabilitation should improve and the organization and standard of services offered by the health establishments should be raised.

The unified system of *rest and recreation* set up in recent years has not yet fully displayed its advantages. It is necessary to enhance the role of the trade unions, and also to promote the interest of departments and organization in the building, management and utilization of the facilities. It is an important task to improve the organization and conditions of the daily rest and weekend recreation of the working people, and make special efforts to provide holiday camps and vacations for children and students.

We acclaim the achievements of our sportsmen and women at international events. Along with that we should reemphasize the fact that we attach prime importance to *mass physical training and sports;* they are essential to the harmonious development of the individual, they are also the main prerequisite for high sporting achievements. Consequently, it is necessary to give decisive priority to the construction of light sports facilities at enterprises and schools and in residential areas.

2. ENVIRONMENT

The further improvement of the socialist lifestyle calls for the uninterrupted improvement of the *environment*. This is a complex problem which covers the planning of towns and villages, living conditions, conditions for work and rest, family and social milieu and the natural environment.

It is high time that a lucid conception for the development of *the network of inhabited localities* was worked out. Planning should be carried out of settlements that together form a unified system, in which the material and technical facilities of the production sphere and the services are constructed for the needs of the system of settlements as a whole rather than for each individual one. This approach will bring considerable savings of time and money, it will contribute to the better regulation of the migration processes and will reflect on the development of the big cities.

More than 242,000 *houses and flats* were built in Bulgaria during the Sixth Five-year Plan period. The per capita floor space is now 13.3 sq. m. In spite of the obvious progress, the housing problem is not yet solved, especially in the big cities and industrial areas.

The Central Committee regards the housing problems as

a strategic problem of our social policy and proposes to adopt a course of its overall accelerated solution. We should set ourselves the task of building 400,000 houses and flats during the Seventh Five-year Plan. The implementation of this task calls for enlisting the efforts of the workforces and the public organizations and for expanding the scale of group-and-cooperative and individual construction. More attention should be paid to the updating of existing housing. It is necessary to make maximum use of the housing stock in the villages by resolving the transportation problem of those who commute.

It is necessary to improve decisively *production and social conditions of work.* Special measures are to be taken to increase the production of technical equipment for the drive against noise and air pollution, for diminishing vibrations, for improving lighting, doing away with or rendering harmless noxious waste, etc. Special attention should be devoted to the working conditions of women with a view to protecting their functions of mothers of healthy children.

Particular measures have been taken for the preservation of the *environment* during the period following the Tenth Congress. The advantages of the socialist system in this sphere were not made full use of, however. The development of the economy will involve the commissioning of productions which pollute the environment. Therefore, a new approach should be adopted in the work to preserve the environment; damage should be prevented and other violations should not be permitted, the comprehensive approach should be applied so as to ensure, in the words of Marx, harmonious relations between society and nature. In this connection, the rights and responsibilities of the respective state and public bodies should be increased.

The drive for raising the people's material well-being, for the ever fuller satisfaction of the growing demand for goods and services, for improving the living environment – this is not a 'consumerist approach' nor a 'lapse into a bourgeois way of life'. To us, to our Party, these are *preconditions for the health and life expectancy of the people, for the all-round physical and cultural development of the individual.*

3. CHANGES IN THE STRUCTURE OF SOCIETY AND THE DEVELOPMENT OF SOCIALIST DEMOCRACY

Comrades,
One of the main tasks of the Party after the Tenth Congress was to expand the participation of the people's masses in the country's administration, to extend and enrich socialist democracy on the basis of the changes in the structure of society.

The working class continued to grow in strength after the Tenth Congress.The number of workers increased by nearly half a million and reached 57 per cent of the working population as against 47 per cent in 1970. The infrastructure of the working class, its qualitative composition has been improved. The absolute and relative number of workers engaged in machine-building, especially in electronics, metallurgy and chemistry, has increased. A number of trades involving hard, unskilled labour employed fewer people, and in some cases were completely done away with. In 1975 the highly skilled workers in industry, construction and transport represented 33.8 per cent, the semi-skilled workers – 47.7 per cent, the unskilled workers – 18.5 per cent. As a result of mechanization and automation, by raising the level of education and improving the technical qualifications of the workers and of young people with secondary and higher education joining their ranks, the tendency towards a gradual promotion of the working class to the level of the engineering and technical intelligentsia is growing stronger.

Considerable changes have taken place in the *class of the cooperative farmers*. In 1974 the proportion of the cooperative farmers fell to 15 per cent of those working in the national economy, as against 28 per cent in 1970. At the same time the number of machine operators and technicians increased significantly. In the agro-industrial complexes the mentality of the cooperative farmers, who are coming ever closer to the working class, continued to change.

The socialist intelligentsia underwent further development. Parallel with its quantitative growth, considerable qualitative changes also occurred. That part of the intelligentsia which directly guides production and develops and introduces scientific and technological achievements marked a particularly rapid increase. The number increased and the role was enhanced of the scientific, teaching and artistic intelligentsia which creates cultural values and plays an important role in the formation of the socialist personality. Changes have taken place not only in the number, but also in the character of work and the role of those engaged in administrative and managerial activities, in the finance and crediting establishments, etc.

The changes that have taken place in production and social relations, the process of bringing closer together the nature of labour, lifestyle, culture and mentality of the cooperative farmers and of the working class and the gradual bridging of the gap between them, on the one hand, and the intelligentsia, on the other, reveal new opportunities for the development of socialist democracy, for consolidating the socialist way of life.

Over the last few years, *the unified system of public administration* has been improved in accordance with the present stage of development of society and the achievements of the scientific and technological revolution. As our experience has shown, the overstaffed system inevitably leads to red tape and does not provide profitable and effective leadership, as a result of which we are passing over to a two-tier and three-tier system of management. Our aim is to simplify and reduce the costs of public administration and to raise the competency, efficiency and effectiveness of management. We should never forget that the main task in public administration is and will be the guidance of the people and of the workforces.

The high degree of socialization of production, its concentration and intensification, the centralized management of large territorial units may lead to the Party and economic management becoming separated from people, divorced from the problems of their life, from everything that moves and concerns them. That is why, in improving administration, the Party looks for and applies new forms and ways of expanding and intensifying the participation of the working people in the solution of social problems, and develops *socialist democracy*.

The application of the *state-cum-public and public-cum-state principle* has become one of the most important trends in the development of public administration. The forms of *direct and representative participation by the workers and cooperative farmers in the management of the economic organizations* have been further developed. The general meetings, the meetings of representatives, the economic committees and economic councils offer real opportunities for a regular and active participation by the workers and cooperative farmers in management and, along with this, increase their responsibility for the fulfilment of the decisions taken. After the Tenth Congress, a *new and original form of direct democracy – the workforce extension plan* – appeared and developed, based on Lenin's ideas. Through it millions of people directly create a better organization of production and reveal additional opportunities for the growth of labour productivity, for the more rapid raising of the standard of living.

During the period under review, *the democratic development of the state bodies* was expressed mainly in the improvement of their organization and in the content of their activity. The representative bodies were formed and acted in accordance with the requirements of the new Constitution.

The *National Assembly* more systematically discussed and adopted decisions on the basic problems of the country's home and foreign policy, and also, directly or through the standing commissions, exercised control over the respective ministries and departments. Its international activities expanded. It is necessary that the National Assembly should continue the process of renovating and refining legislation and that it should intensify its control over the executive state bodies.

The *State Council*, formed as a new organ embodying Lenin's idea of the unity of power worked out a number of strategic problems of state administration in accordance with the Party policy. The principle of uniting the state and public principle in the country's administration was creatively developed in its activity through the participation of representatives of the political and mass organizations, of eminent scientists and men of culture and the arts in the councils with the State Council. The State Council should still more fully avail itself of the authority which it is invested with by the new Constitution in the elaboration of strategic decisions and in its control over the execution of the laws and of the decisions it has taken.

The *Council of Ministers* made efforts to reorganize its work in the spirit of the Party Programme and the new Constitution and in keeping with the changes that have taken place in the system of public administration and the tasks of the country's socio-economic development. In order to become a viable supreme executive and competent body of state power, the Council of Ministers should relieve itself of extrinsic functions. It should take up and more successfully implement the strategic tasks of our development, increase the initiative and efficiency of the ministries and its other organs and particularly intensify the control over the fulfilment of the normative acts passed by the National Assembly and the State Council and of its own decisions.

The people's councils have also improved their work. They take an active part in the elaboration and fulfilment of the plans for the socio-economic development of the respective administrative and territorial units, for improving the public services, for ever more fully satisfying the material and cultural needs of the population.

The courts of justice, the prosecutor's office and the Ministry of the Interior are successfully fighting against violations of the law. In the future, besides regional judges, district judges will be elected directly by the population. The prosecutor's office and the courts are faced with the task of improving their work for unconditional observance of socialist legality on the basis of the equality of all citizens before the law.

The Bulgarian People's Army grew stronger and ever more firmly established itself as an unvanquishable force in defence of our socialist homeland and as a true school for communist education and the physical tempering of young men, for forming in them military and civic virtues. That is why our Party and people lavish great care and attention on their army. The Party, as heretofore, will constantly raise the fighting trim of the army and will increase the defence capability of the state within the framework of the Warsaw Treaty Organization.

After the Tenth Congress, the Central Committee did a considerable amount of theoretical and practical work for enhancing the role of *the public organizations and movements*.

The Fatherland Front reorganized its activity. Developing as heretofore as the largest public-cum-political organization and a national movement, the Fatherland Front should use more efficient forms for improving socialist democracy, for consolidating the ties between state bodies and particularly between the people's councils and the population, and should contribute to the development of public control. It should work for the class-and-Party, patriotic and internationalist education of the population, for creating a sound socio-psychological climate in the residential areas, for enhancing the role of the family and society in the communist education of the growing generation.

The Party's Central Committee worked out a concept for the place and role of *the Bulgarian Trade Unions*. Of prime importance in their work were the problems of the socio-political and labour activity of industrial and office workers, the latter's participation in the management of production and the country's administration. The organization and leadership of socialist emulation, the ideological, political and mass cultural work have been improved. The trade unions should make fuller use of their possibilities of enhancing the role of production conferences, workers' meetings, and the collective labour contracts; they should increase public and labour activity, especially during the formation and fulfilment of the workforce extension plans; they should wage a struggle against negative phenomena and sentiments, and in defence of the class and personal interests of the workers. Much care should be taken in the selection and training of leading trade union cadres, more daring steps should be taken to promote production workers to leading trade union posts.

The role and importance of *the movement of Bulgarian women* have been growing. We should stress, with good reason, the interest, activity and perseverance with which the Committee and the councils of women point to unsolved problems and assist the Party and state bodies in providing comprehensive conditions for coordinating woman's functions as a mother, worker and public figure, for the all-round development of her personality. The Party once again expresses its profound gratitude to the Bulgarian women for their great contribution to our all-round socialist development. The further enhancement of the role of women is a task of the whole society and an inseparable part of our economic and social policy.

The activity of the *Dimitrov Young Communist League* during the period under review proceeded in the spirit of the Theses of the Party's Central Committee on Youth and the Decisions of the Tenth Congress of the Bulgarian Communist Party. Work on the ideological, patriotic, internationalist, and military and technical education and training of youth was substantially improved. The contribution of the younger generation to socialist construction and especially to the development of the promising sectors of the economy increased. The movement of scientific and technical creative work of young people is developing successfully. Generally speaking, comrades, our Dimitrov Komsomol, which continues and develops in the new conditions, the revolutionary traditions of its glorious predecessors, is a worthy assistant and reserve force of the Bulgarian Communist Party. Our Party and people are rightfully proud of their Komsomol, of their inspired young people loyal to communism.

Serious weaknesses and shortcomings, however, still exist in the organizational work and in the life of the Komsomol committees and societies and these negatively influence their work to form a Marxist-Leninist outlook and communist virtues in young people.

We are concerned, for instance, at the consumerist attitude towards life, the desire for philistine prosperity, the disregard for labour of some young people. The consumption figures for alcohol and cigarettes are growing. Quite often there is tolerance of vices and anti-social deeds. The overwhelming majority of our young people are offspring of the socialist system, they are young people with bright intellects and pure souls, they are ideologically and morally strong. But the Komsomol leaderships do not always manage to rely upon them so that they may create public intolerance of deeds which are, in their essence, an expression of bourgeois views, of bourgeois morality.

There are still phenomena of the so-called 'petty justice' in our life. Young people are more deeply pained than are adults by injustice, indifference, self-seeking, unscrupulous mentality. It is more difficult for young people to tell the important from the unimportant, the typical from the atypical, to tell which is new and victorious and which is doomed to disappear under the blows of our social development. Left on his own, an adolescent may form false ideas about life, society, and human nature. The Komsomol which has done a great deal for the communist education of youth, should shape in the young people a scientific outlook and spiritual stability, irreconcilability to violations of the moral and humane norms of the socialist way of life, and which should enlist them for active participation in the building of the new and just socialist society.

The question of the conditions in which young people spend their leisure, of what places they have for rest and entertainment, for talking and making friends should be raised openly and unmistakenly. Without beating about the bush, we must admit that, in spite of the decisions and decrees, we have done very little in this respect. Lately we have been alarmed by the growing number of divorces and we blame young people for their frivolous attitude towards such serious matters as marriage and family life, their indifference to the fate of the children deprived of a father or a mother. The personal responsibility should not be belittled. But is it not time for us to see that one of the reasons for the unsuccessful marriages and for a number of negative phenomena lies in the shortcomings allowed in the formation of the new lifestyle?

In the past, when Bulgaria was a country with a patriarchal way of life, in every village there was a square where on high days and holidays lively chain-dances were performed. There were working bees where girls and young men met. There were gatherings where young and old alike came from all over the area. The rapid pace at which we have reorganized our agriculture and industrialized our country has shifted around the population. The old villages and small provincial towns in which all the people knew one another, exist no more. The old patriarchal way of life was too poor, too narrow for us to feel sorry about its passing. But the new lifestyle has not yet properly taken shape so that we may feel satisfied and untroubled. We are hurrying to catch up with the advanced countries and build one factory after another. The migration processes created acute housing problems. And now we are hurrying to build new housing estates. New districts are being built in the old towns, new towns spring up. But what happens? Often these large housing estates lag behind to no small extent in the availability of services to the population – shops, coffee shops, cinemas, library clubs, sports grounds etc.

Young people are brought up and shaped as personalities in the family, the school, the Komsomol and the workforce. Their leisure time activities are also of great importance. Young people love sports and entertainment. If we do not create favourable conditions for them, they will look for them somewhere else. And then much of what we have built up can be destroyed or weakened.

The question of the utilization of leisure time, of the proper organization of the rest and recreation of young people must now become one of the greatest concerns of the Komsomol. Naturally, this task cannot be solved through the efforts and with the possibilities of the Komsomol alone. It is also our task – a task of the Party, state and public bodies and organizations, of the economic and administrative leaderships. Over the last few years wonderful houses for the youth, real palaces, have sprung up in some district centres. Palaces are a nice thing. But is it not better to build for the time being more modest but larger numbers of youth clubs? Some public catering establishments should be put at the disposal of young people, establishments where young people may dance, where alcoholic drinks are not served and there is no smoking, establishments where young people are not obliged to order food and where no profits are made. Quite a few canteens exist at offices and factories which in the evenings may be used as youth clubs. In those places, where there are no such facilities, youth clubs should be built with all of society taking part and first of all with the young people themselves contributing their energy and work.

Or let us take, for instance, the school and the student brigades. They render useful and often indisputable help to agriculture. But what about the educational aspect of this movement? We can say outright: grave shortcomings are being allowed here. The Komsomol has to take measures to include in the leaderships of the brigades only the best young people, who, with their diligence and initiative, with their good morals, adherence to principles and comradely concern, will be an example to follow!

We have young generations to whom we can confidently entrust the future of communism in Bulgaria. It is our duty, the duty of the Bulgarian Communist Party and the Dimitrov Young Communist League to the future of our homeland, to constantly raise the level of ideological and educational work and to instil in our young people the invaluable qualities and virtues of the man of the communist society!

Comrades,

The joint work of the Party with the Bulgarian Agrarian Party was further developed after the Tenth Congress.

Recently the BAP celebrated its 75th anniversary. Together with our comrades from the BAP, we marked the 50th anniversary of the days when the sound basis of the cooperation between the BCP and the left-wing forces in the BAP was laid.

Disunited and pitted against each other, the communists and agrarians were defeated by monarcho-fascist reaction in 1923. The alliance between them became a historic necessity for overthrowing the bourgeois rule. After the victory of September 9, 1944, the alliance between the BCP and the BAP did not weaken, but grew stronger. The process of socialist construction brought about radical transformations in the structure of society. The Bulgarian Agrarian Party, however, exists and will continue to exist, since it does fruitful work of great use to the people in the new conditions, in the conditions of building a developed socialist society in Bulgaria. The communists' attitude towards their allies is eloquently illustrated by a paragraph in the new Constitution of the People's Republic of Bulgaria, which proclaims that 'The Bulgarian Communist Party heads the construction of a developed socialist society in the People's Republic of Bulgaria in close, fraternal cooperation with the Bulgarian Agrarian Party.'

At this congress we reaffirm our loyalty to the fraternal friendship and cooperation between communists and agrarians and acclaim the all-round activity of the BAP in building socialism in the villages, as well as its activity on the international scene in rallying the agrarian and democratic parties and movements in the struggle for peace, democracy and social progress.

4. ART AND CULTURE, THE MASS MEDIA AND THE ESTABLISHMENT OF THE SOCIALIST LIFESTYLE

Comrades,
Our Party has repeatedly emphasized the great, unique role of literature and art in the many-sided activity aimed at the education of the new man, at the establishment of the socialist lifestyle. Naturally, this role can be played only by such literature and art which, in Lenin's words, are part of the common proletarian cause, part of the Party work; by such literature and art which are indissolubly linked with the people, which are familiar with the Party's policy and its practical activity, which view the problems and trends of social development from class and Party positions and, in their own specific medium, take an interested, active and inspired part in the drive for building the socialist society, for the victory of communism.

Eighteen years ago the Central Committee launched the appeal: 'Closer to the people, closer to life!' Now we can say with gratification that the last few years and especially the period between the two congresses have witnessed a turn from a more or less isolated to a mass orientation of creative artists towards the problems of socialist reality. The best representatives of our artistic intelligentsia created works which reflect realistically and with great professional skill, the fundamental processes of life and the formation of the new man. These works – valuable acquisitions of the Bulgarian socialist art and culture – are a confirmation of the correctness and fruitfulness of the April 1956 policy of our Party, of the Leninist principles of guidance of literature and the arts, and of the method of socialist realism.

At the same time it should be clearly pointed out that the breakthrough observed in the orientation towards the problems of the present day has not yet brought about a breakthrough in the mastering of the contemporary subject matter in all its historical scope and significance. The striving towards a truthful, communist art devoted to the Party is a fact; so is the striving to create ideologically and artistically significant works about our times. There are real talents among all generations of creative artists. Obviously, the chief obstacles on the way towards the realization of the good intentions and aspirations are the insufficient knowledge of life and the underestimation of the drive for high creative skill.

What is pleasing about all this is the growing awareness which the individual artists, their unions and the Committee for Art and Culture as a public-cum-state body are showing of these shortcomings. In the last few years the district Party and state leaderships have rendered substantial assistance in bringing the creative artists closer to life – a new phenomenon indicative of the deep interest which our society takes in the creation of significant artistic works on contemporary subjects.

We expect from the Bulgarian artistic and cultural intelligentsia – the Party's loyal and talented detachment – to strengthen and deepen its ties with the life of the working people and improve their mastery so as to delight us with works which recreate our times sweepingly and brilliantly and which, with ardent devotion to the Party, assert the socialist lifestyle – synonymous with the overall superiority of the socialist system over capitalism, works, which will be an invincible weapon in the struggle for the triumph of the communist ideas and ideals in the minds and hearts of millions of people in our country and throughout the world!

The creation of national artistic values and the transfer of artistic values created by other nations into our country is not an end in itself. The artistic values must reach the greatest possible number of people, must become part of their knowledge and enrich them ideologically and intellectually. With the coordinating role of the Committee for Art and Culture and the participation of all cultural and public organizations and state institutions a considerable amount of work was done to this purpose and the groundwork was laid for drafting a *Programme for nationwide aesthetic education*. Now efforts have to be aimed at *forming a truly nationwide movement for aesthetic education, at organizing the educational work in aesthetics, which should be rich in content and varied in form and should provide opportunities for the active aesthetic contribution of all age groups in the process of all human activities.*

We could not conceive of our work on moulding the socialist personality, on the development of the socialist lifestyle, without the active participation of *the mass media*. The press, the television, the radio, the information agencies and book publishing are the main channels for spreading spiritual values and for mass political influence. They not only offer information about events in the country and abroad, not only reflect the achievements of the people, but also take a direct part in organizing them. 85 central and district newspapers with a total circulation of more than 5 million are now published in our country, as well as 207 magazines with a circulation of 3.2 million. 19,900 books were published with a total circulation of 230 million. The number of TV sets topped the 1.5 million mark, that of radio sets, transistor radios and radio-rediffusion sets reached the figure of 2.7 million; the television and radio have 5 to 6 million viewers and listeners each.

Now the task is to *raise higher the ideological and especially the professional and creative level of the mass media.* The main condition for that is the proper selection and systematic training of the *journalistic, editorial and publishing cadres*, regarded by the Party as responsible ideological workers, as its close aides. It is also necessary to overcome the lagging behind in the development of *the material and technical base of the mass media*. New printing facilities were built for the Georgi Dimitrov State Printing House during the five-year period, and the Balkan Printing House was commissioned and equipped with the most up-to-date machines. The construction of a national radio-television centre began last year. A ground space station is being built for linking the country to the Intersputnik system. The question of building the up-to-date Rabot-nichesko Delo newspaper complex has been resolved. During the Seventh Five-year Plan the entire territory of the country has to be covered by a powerful radio and television signal. The problem of the paper supply has to be solved with a view to the future.

Here, from this rostrum, we should like to reiterate the Central Committee's high appraisal of the correct class and Party stand of our journalists, of their active contribution to the country's socialist construction, to the establishment of the socialist lifestyle.

5. BRIEFLY ABOUT RIGHTS AND OBLIGATIONS

Comrades,

It is known that in class societies the state is an instrument of the ruling class and no bourgeois democratic forms of government can change this fact. The socialist state, from its very beginning, even at its most rudimentary stage, is incomparably more democratic than the most developed bourgeois democracy, since it is the power of the working class in alliance with the broadest working masses, it is the power of the class which is out to build a classless communist society rather than to perpetuate its own domination. Freedom and democracy – real freedom and democracy – can exist only where there are no exploiters or exploited, where the means of production are public, and not private property. True democracy, democracy for the majority of the people is ushered in with the victory of the socialist revolution. Its development is an objective corollary of the development of the socialist system and, at the same time, a pre-condition for the further development of society along the road of socialism and communism.

In addition to granting citizens all rights and freedoms, socialist democracy provides real guarantees for them. At the same time it implies the requirement that every citizen fulfils his or her obligations to society on an equal footing. This is a sine qua non and a precondition for the further development and deepening of socialist democracy as an intrinsic feature of the socialist lifestyle.

The dialectics of development is such that the socialist lifestyle is not established overnight, neither is it something set and immutable. Lenin pointed out that every society invariably contains vestiges of the past, the groundwork of the present and the embryos of the future. The development of the new lifestyle takes place in the conditions of irreconcilable struggle against the remnants of the past, and for the ever fuller expression of the new lifestyle's inherent features and an all-round stimulation of the germs of the future.

In this connection, *the question of the socialist attitude towards labour deserves particular attention.*

To interpret socialist lifestyle and its development solely in the terms of scope and rates of satisfying the material and cultural needs of the people is a one-sided and utterly erroneous approach. In actual fact, *socialist labour – this most significant form of human activity – is the pith of the socialist lifestyle, its essential feature.* This is labour free from exploitation and random economic development welding together personal and public interests, it is labour through which the socialist personality asserts itself and gains wide scope for the manifestation of its physical and intellectual abilities.

Our society is a working society. It has been built and develops thanks to the united, honest and constructive labour of the people. Everything in this world – from the loaf of bread to the work of art – is the fruit of man's labour. To add his work to the work of the people is a matter of duty and honour for every member of our society, so that he or she can have the right and the privilege to say: this is my world!

IV. THE STATE AND TASKS OF THE PARTY

Comrades,

All our successes are closely connected with the state and activity of the Party, with its ability to put forward and tackle the urgent problems. We can declare with a feeling of deep satisfaction that, equipped with the Programme adopted at the Tenth Congress, our Bulgarian Communist Party has proved once again that it is a worthy vanguard of the Bulgarian working class and leader of the Bulgarian people.

During the whole period under review, our Party – from the Central Committee to the local organizations and their committees – has made consistent efforts to organize and pursue its activity in the spirit of the decisions of the Tenth Congress, to apply a correct, Leninist style of work and leadership, to consolidate and develop the collective method of work, to use a political and scientific approach, enthusiasm and efficiency, and to rely on the masses.

The general and election meetings and conferences before the Congress clearly showed the maturity, cohesion and strength of the Party. They took stock of the achievements and weaknesses in a businesslike and self-critical manner and seriously and profoundly discussed the forthcoming tasks. The communists un-animously approved the Marxist-Leninist policy of the Party, the stand it has, taken in the international communist movement, as well as the activity of the Central Committee and its Politburo, and the foreign policy of the country. Our Party is closely rallied and united from top to bottom, from the Central Committee to the local Party organizations. It is firmly convinced that the way along which we are marching is the only right way. It is full of resolution to work for the further implementation and development of the April policy, for the realization of the Programme for building a developed socialist society in Bulgaria.

The tasks which the Eleventh Congress will set before the country will make new demands, above all, on the leading Party, on its committees and organizations, on its cadres, on all communists.

Allow me to dwell briefly on some topical and important problems of Party organizational and ideological work.

1. IMPROVING THE COMPOSITION OF THE PARTY

Improving the quantitative and qualitative composition of the Party is our prime, our invariable concern.

Since the Tenth Congress, the Party has grown by 90,320 people and now totals 789,796 members organized in 28,850 locals. The quantitative growth was accompanied by a number of positive qualitative changes. The workers, who account for 41.4 per cent of the membership, are in the frontline of the Party. The number of women has increased and they now form 27.5 per cent of the membership and 36.5 per cent of the newly admitted members. We are also happy to note that nearly three-quarters of the newly admitted Party members are young people under 30. About 70 per cent of the communists employed in the national economy, work in material production, and almost every third engineer and technician is a member of the Party.

Efforts to further improve the composition of the Party in a qualitative respect are now coming to the fore.

The Central Committee decided *to replace the Party membership cards* after the Congress. The replacement of the membership cards is an important political, ideological and organizational undertaking and should serve the purpose of a review of our militant ranks. It should help to increase the activeness and responsibility of the communists, to raise their Marxist-Leninist consciousness, their discipline in and principled attitude to production, and public and everyday life. We are not carrying through a purge. But in replacing the membership cards, the Party organizations should decisively rid themselves of members who violate the Programme and Statutes of the Party, who transgress the Party principles and norms, the socialist laws, and whose behaviour undermines the political and moral prestige of the Bulgarian Communist Party.

2. FURTHER RAISING THE ROLE OF THE LOCAL PARTY ORGANIZATIONS AND THE LOCAL PARTY ORGANS

Our second, particularly important task is to further enhance the importance and role of the local Party organizations and the local Party organs. The local Party organizations are everywhere – in the plants, in the institutes, on the construction sites, in the villages, in the city districts. Through them, the Party feels the pulse of the many-sided life, and through them it pursues its daily political, organizational and ideological-educational work among the working people for the implementation of its policy.

During the period under review, the Party organizations were strengthened ideologically and organizationally, and have improved their activity. They deal concretely and competently with the most important problems of production and of the social life of the workforces, they lead a regular inner Party life and exercise their right of control over the administrative and economic managements. Naturally, there are still organizations whose presence in the workforce is not sufficiently felt. The higher Party bodies should take prompt measures in this respect. Our main task now is to further improve the work of all Party organizations, including those which function well, to raise their role of leading political nuclei of the workforces, to establish them as a prototype of the future workforce.

This can only be achieved by further developing *inner Party life* on the basis of the Leninist norms and principles, of the requirements of the Programme and Statutes of the Party. The Party's strength lies in the conscious discipline of its members, based on inner conviction. That is why it is necessary considerably to improve *the individual work with the communists*. By developing inner Party democracy and the free exchange of views in the spirit of the Party Statutes, the Party organization, the Party collective should constantly help the individual communist to grow into an organizer and educator of the masses, into a person whose whole activity and behaviour introduce a Party spirit, class consciousness and communist morality in the workforce in which he works and with which he lives. The individual work with the communists is extremely important in strengthening mutual trust and the unity of the living chain of 'leaders – Party – working class – people'.

We, the Bulgarian communists, have good reason to be proud of our Party. Today the task is for the Party organizations to work with the individual communists in such a way that the Party should be proud of each of its members!

Comrades,

The Central Committee of the Party has always highly valued the role of the *local Party organs* and has taken care to strengthen them and to improve their organizational activity. The district, town and other local Party committees have developed and become competent and authoritative organs of political leadership and their contribution to the all-round development of the material and spiritual life of the people has been generally acknowledged. They enjoy not only the trust of the Party organizations and of the Central Committee, but also the trust and gratitude of the masses of working people.

Stress is now laid on the efforts of the district committees to reinforce the *municipal Party committees* with cadres, to place their activity on correct foundations, and turn them into real political leaders of the all-round life in the municipalities.

At the present stage, great importance is attached to the problems of *the style and methods of work of the local Party organs, of their apparatus and cadre.*

It is necessary even more clearly *to distinguish between the functions* of the local Party organs, particularly of the district and town ones, and the functions of the bodies of public administration. The task of the Party organs is not to duplicate, but to assure conditions for developing the initiative of the state, economic and public bodies and organizations, to strengthen their sense of responsibility for the state of the work in their sectors and their self-confidence as leaders.

The many-sided activity of the Party is becoming ever more complex. It is no longer possible to guide competently without constantly raising the *scientific level* of the work of the Party apparatus, without improving *planning* and the *collective approach* to analysis, conclusions and decisions-making.

The drive for implementing decisions is now the main condition for raising the quality and effectiveness of Party organizational work. Control of implementation is a characteristic feature of the Leninist style of leadership. We should constantly improve not only our ability to take correct decisions, but also our ability to control and demand, to carry through the work undertaken. In this respect it is necessary to ensure *closer interaction between the Party organs, including the auditing commissions of the Party, and the bodies of the Committee for State and People's Control.* The need to extend the scope and raise exigence in the work of state and people's control is one aspect of the problem. The other aspect is the Party control over the state, economic and public bodies, which should eliminate the weaknesses and irregularities observed.

By their competence and exigence, by their ability to rely on the cadres and the working people, by the overall style of their work, the Party committees should increasingly become a model for all bodies of public administration.

3. ON CADRE POLICY AND THE TRAINING OF CADRES

Comrades,

During the period under review, the Central Committee and the local Party committees educated, trained and promoted to leading posts a *considerable fresh reinforcement of capable activists* in all sectors of socialist construction. *The April policy of uniting* the cadres of all generations, of trust in them and respect for their work is persistently being pursued.

We have a high regard and deep respect for the cadres steeled in the decades-long struggle of the Party against capitalism and fascism, for establishing and strengthening the people's rule – cadres who continue

110

today, side by side with the other generations, to devote all their efforts, knowledge and experience to the building of a developed socialist society in our country.

The natural process of renewal and growth of the Party cadres, of reinforcing them with new activists, is guided and managed in the right way.

At the same time we should be clearly aware that, in the selection of cadres, *we do not always observe the requirement for organic unity between the political and the businesslike qualities* and in quite a few cases we tip the balance to one or the other side. Furthermore, we still allow the promotion of people for reasons of kinship or friendship, for having come from the same part of the country, or out of personal loyalty. Mistaken liberalism, tolerating in responsible posts people who have shown that they lack the qualities to hold them, still continue. Weaknesses are also allowed in the fight against the narrowly local and departmental approach in the activity of the cadres, which does harm to society as a whole.

The cadres are the greatest asset of the Party, the people and the country. No matter how conditions change, no matter to what extent technology develops and the cybernetic principles are introduced in management, the Leninist formulation that the cadres decide all, is in force and will always be in force. That is why the Bulgarian Communist Party insists and will continue even more strictly to insist that the Leninist principles of the selection, training and promotion of cadres be abided by, it will assert them as an inviolable guiding principle of cadre policy and activity in all spheres of life and at all levels.

Lenin used to say that *the working class is our main cadre reserve,* because this broad stratum possesses a proletarian instinct, a proletarian sense of duty. The worker of today possesses also general and special knowledge, which brings him near to the level of the scientific and technical cadres. Consequently, we can and must more confidently promote to responsible posts the best representatives of the most progressive and most numerous class in our society.

To enable the cadres to develop all their powers and abilities, it is particularly important to assure *consistency in their promotion and stability of their position.* Greater attention should be given to *the cadres who have had experience in local practical work* at the plants and agro-industrial complexes, in the local Party and state bodies. This approach should be combined with the *democratic principle* of electivity and the gradual introduction of competition in promoting and appointing people to economic and administrative posts, also taking into account the opinion of the workforce and the point of view of the Party organization. Only in this way can we guard against the harmful consequences of subjectivism, of haste, of accidentally promoting cadres – a danger to which, as life has shown, we are not immune.

The Party will continue in future to accord its cadres trust and respect; it will help raise their self-confidence and enhance their prestige. Trust and respect, however, are inseparable from the personal responsibility of the cadres for the work they are entrusted with. They are earned and maintained by the cadres' overall activity, and are not given once and for all, as 'dowry' for past services. *Exigence* is also a necessary condition for the growth of the cadres themselves. Lack of exigence and irresponsibility are the main reason why we still have in our country activists who turn haughty and presumptuous, who violate Party morality and the law, and abuse the confidence they enjoy, the rights they have been granted and the power they have been entrusted with. No mistaken liberalism and no indulgence should be shown toward such people. They should be *resolutely removed from their leading posts,* and that should be done not only in the interest of the work, but also in the interest of the correct education of cadres.

In their work with the cadres, regardless of the sector to which they have been posted, the Party committees and Party organizations should even more persistently cultivate a strong sense of responsibility before the Party and society — responsibility for their personal actions and for the workforce of which they are in charge; a creative attitude to problems, initiative, enthusiasm and a businesslike approach, intolerance to routine and stagnation, constant concern for improving their professional, political and general knowledge; unity between words and actions, modesty and simplicity in their behaviour, and a natural manner in their contacts with people.

Our Party has a large   army of loyal, highly skilled, energetic and authoritative leaders of a socialist type, united and serried in their ranks around the Central Committee, capable of successfully translating the Party decisions into life. To them the Central Committee and our entire Party express their full confidence and their gratitude for their honest and devoted work, for their great share in the respect and love with which our people surround the Bulgarian Communist Party!

4. FOR MILITANT AND EFFECTIVE IDEOLOGICAL WORK

Comrades,

The period after the Tenth Congress was particularly fruitful for the ideological work of the Party. The programme-task of creating a science-based strategy of ideological work at the stage of building a developed socialist society was fulfilled. A many-sided drive was launched for restructuring ideological work and linking it most closely with the tasks of socialist construction and the education of the new man.

In spite of the progress made, a number of weaknesses still exist in the ideological work of the Party. Further energetic efforts are evidently needed in order to carry through its reconstruction.

Our Party has always attached special importance to the theoretical training of its members, to the mastering of the Marxist-Leninist theory, without which communists cannot fulfil their vanguard role in socialist construction and in the struggle against bourgeois ideology. We have a tried and tested system of improving the Marxist-Leninist education of the communists and non-Party activists, and a streamlined system of economic training of executive and managerial cadres has been functioning for two years. Nearly 940,000 communists and non-Party members have taken part in the system of Party education during the current academic year, and over 1 million people in the system of economic training.

What is needed now?

It is necessary to raise the ideological and

theoretical standard of the propaganda of Marxism-Leninism by improving the theoretical and methodological training of the propagandists and by increasing the individual study of the works of the classics of Marxism-Leninism, of the documents of the congresses and plenary sessions.

The study of Marxism-Leninism should be closely linked with the policy of the Party and the practical tasks of the workforces, with the topical home and international events, with the history and experience of our Party and the international communist movement.

It is necessary to devote special care to the Marxist-Leninist instruction and education of the young communists and the members of the Dimitrov Young Communist League from among whom the Party, the socialist state and the public organizations recruit their future cadres.

The drive for the fulfilment of the socio-economic programme of the Seventh Five-year Plan should become the centre of the mass political work. The organization, content, forms and methods of political propaganda work should be directed towards one goal: the main strategic task of raising sharply the effectiveness of the economy and the quality of production should become a personal cause of each worker. This requires a great deal of political and explanatory work not only among the workforces but also among individual workers.

Technocratic attitudes, underestimation of the ideological and political content of economic and administrative work should be resolutely dealt with. Whenever important decisions concerning the interests of the broad masses are to be taken, their political and educational effect should be considered in advance, and measures should be envisaged to elucidate them.

The participation of leading Party, economic and administrative cadres, of all communists in explaining the tasks both in general campaigns and in individual work and daily contacts with the people is of paramount importance for the success of mass political work. No underestimation of the personal work with the individual workers should be allowed. There is no shorter way to the heart and soul of man than the personal contact and heart-to-heart talk.

Our ideological front as a whole faces an old, but never outdated task of exceptional importance: *to wage an uncompromising, offensive struggle against bourgeois ideology.* Life constantly confirms the correctness of this principle as formulated by the great Lenin: 'The question can be posed *in this way only:* bourgeois or socialist ideology! There is no other alternative... That is why *any* underestimation of the socialist ideology, *any deviation* from it means also the strengthening of bourgeois ideology.' (V. I. Lenin, Works, Vol. 5, pp. 398-399, Bulgarian edition). As it was stated in the Programme of our Party, the struggle between the   ideologies is increasingly becoming at present one of the strategic bridgeheads of the class struggle, of the duel between the two worlds.

The importance of the ideological struggle grows parallel with the establishment of peaceful coexistence between states with different social systems. Having been compelled to reconcile itself to the change in the balance of power, *imperialism seeks revenge in the sphere of ideological struggle.* It tries to warp the socialist public conscience in our countries, to foment nationalism, anti-Sovietism and opportunism in its various shades in order to break the unity of the world communist and workers' movement and the front of the anti-imperialist forces.

We shall oppose ever more resolutely these tactics of the imperialist propaganda by improving the work of and the coordination between all ideological sectors, thoroughly and promptly investigating the actions of the enemy and opposing to them the communist views, the successes of the really existing socialism and the advantages of the socialist lifestyle.

The struggle against the ideological adversaries is most effective when *the topical problems of socialist construction and the international development* are elaborated in due time from the positions of creative Marxism-Leninism. We expect from our social scientists to make still greater efforts in studying the fundamental political, economic, social and ideological problems of our development, the problems of building the material and technical base of socialism and international socialist integration, the development of social relations, the formation of a unified all people's socialist ownership, the socio-class changes, the enhanced leading role of the working class and the communist party, the education of the new man. We need profound research into the problems of the scientific and technological revolution and its consequences, into public administration, the improvement of the socialist lifestyle, the struggle against bourgeois ideology and against the anti-Marxist and non-Marxist views. Special care is necessary for the development of *Marxist-Leninist philosophy* as a most general methodology, for the philosophical elaboration of the problems of the construction of the new society, of the problems of man and his relation to society, and the laws of the contemporary period.

The struggle between the communist and the bourgeois ideology is not confined within the boundaries of individual countries. That is why *we hail as a great success the strengthening of ideological cooperation between the countries of the socialist community.*

The ideological front in Bulgaria – from the social sciences to literature and the arts – is monolithic and closely rallied around the Party and its Central Committee. With its irresistible influence on the minds and hearts of the people and of the younger generation in particular, it makes an invaluable contribution to the Party's work and struggle for the building of the developed socialist society, for the education of the new human individual. In close cooperation with the ideological fronts of the Soviet Union and the other fraternal socialist countries, and with the international communist movement, our ideological front participates actively and will continue to participate ever more actively in the joint struggle against bourgeois ideology, in the powerful offensive of the communist ideas throughout the world.

Comrades,
During the period under review the Bulgarian Communist Party scored tremendous successes in all spheres of socialist construction. With its loyalty to Marxism-Leninism and proletarian internationalism, with its creative theoretical,

organizational and guiding activity, with its devotion to the interests of the people, the Bulgarian Communist Party still further established itself as the intellect and motive force of social development, expanded and intensified its links with the working class and all strata of the working people, enhanced its prestige in the international communist and workers' movement and among the broadest progressive circles of the peoples, who are looking for their path towards a new, better and happier life, towards socialism and communism.

From the high rostrum of the Eleventh Congress, the Central Committee expresses its heartfelt gratitude to the powerful army of communists, to the local Party organizations, to the Party committees, to the auditing commissions, to the Party cadres in the state, economic and public bodies and organizations, to all our comrades who, with their devoted work and their whole behaviour, create the strength and the aura of the proud name of *Bulgarian Communist,* the strength and aura of our beloved Bulgarian Communist Party!

V. THE IMMEDIATE HISTORIC TASK OF THE BULGARIAN COMMUNIST PARTY – THE DEVELOPED SOCIALIST SOCIETY AND THE PREPARATION FOR A GRADUAL TRANSITION TO COMMUNISM

Comrades,

With the theses of the Central Committee of the Party, which were published for nationwide discussion before the Eleventh Congress of the Party, an attempt has been made to render concrete the tasks mapped out in the Programme of the Party and to elucidate the development of the economy, scientific and technological progress, the living standards, Party work and some other spheres of the activity of society not only up to 1980, but also for a longer period of time – up to 1990, for instance.

When drawing up the Programme of the Party, we proceeded from the assumption that under favourable international conditions our people will build , in its basic lines, the developed socialist society in the People's Republic of Bulgaria in a period of about 20 years and will then begin the gradual transition to communism. At that time, 5 or 6 years ago, this was only a forecast. Now, when we report on what has been achieved since the Tenth Party Congress and look ahead into the near future, we become convinced that this is an entirely realistic task.

Naturally, none of us entertains   the illusion that

the developed socialist society will be built and the gradual transition to communism will start as a result of the automatic operation of the objective social laws. The construction of mature socialism and the gradual transition to communism are a natural historical process of a gradual passage from a lower to a higher stage of social development. However, the rates of this transition, the choosing of its most efficient forms, ways and means depend to a decisive degree on the subjective factor, on our skill to make maximum use of the advantages of the socialist system, to correctly guide and direct the social processes, to mobilize the efforts, experience and creativity of the working masses.

The perspectives which take shape along our road to communism become and will continue to become a living reality, because the Bulgarian Communist Party, the Party of Dimiter Blagoev and Georgi Dimitrov, the tested militant vanguard of the working class, of all working people in our country, is at the head of the struggle for a better and happier life of the people. These perspectives become and will continue to become a living reality because the Party is armed with the Marxist-Leninist theory, which allows it to elaborate a science-based general policy of development, to lead in a scientific way the all-round social progress. These perspectives become and will continue to become a living reality because the working masses in town and village, who respond with great faith and filial love to the Party of the Bulgarian communists for its loyalty and boundless devotion to the people's interests, are marching confidently with it.

The Party has never kept it secret from the people

that the road which in the not too distant future will lead Bulgaria to the developed socialist society and the gradual transition to communism is not smooth, and that difficulties and obstacles are being and will be encountered on it. The new is always born, grows and gains strength in a struggle with what is old and outdated. Not a single great cause, and still less a cause of such unique greatness in the history of our people can be carried out without overcoming certain difficulties. These are the inevitable difficulties of growth, difficulties which are connected with the lack of sufficient experience or with old ideas and ways of thinking, with inertia and conservatism. The struggle against these difficulties raises still further the responsibility of the Party before the people. Everyone in our country knows that the Bulgarian Communist Party has never shirked its responsibility, has never faltered in the struggle to protect the people's interests. And now our Party, more vigorous than ever and striving ahead, calls on our people to work and fight selflessly for new achievements in the economy, in education and science, in art and culture, in raising material and cultural standards.

The period up to 1990 will be a period of further extensive qualitative and quantitative growth in all spheres of our social development, and it will take us gradually to the building of the material and technical base of socialism, to a further improvement in social relations and the all-round development of the individual. The People's Republic of Bulgaria will in broad outlines become a country of mature socialism, the highest and ultimate stage in the development of socialism as the first phase of the communist socio-economic formation.

In order that this process may proceed in a planned and efficient way, with the greatest economy of time, the latter being of essential significance both from the point of view of internal development and from the point of view of the competition between the two socio-economic systems, it is necessary that the Party and the working people should devote particular care and pay considerable attention to the solution of certain important problems of the construction of the developed socialist society.

The first problem which deserves our particular attention is the problem of completing the construction of the material and technical base of socialism.

It is well known that the material and technical base of socialism continues to be built and undergoes overall development in the process of construction of the mature socialist society. This is one of the objective laws of this phase. The material and technical base of socialism is the determining material prerequisite for the gradual transition to the highest phase of communism. Our country has scored great successes in solving this problem. The efforts should be aimed not only at the powerful development of the national economic complex, but also at new qualitative changes. A task of paramount importance is to ensure further concentration of industrial production and intensification of the national economy, to introduce ever more broadly complex mechanization and automation and, after that, gradually, complex automation as well, and also to introduce new technologies which guarantee high labour productivity. In short, *it is necessary to complete the building and to develop the material and technical base of socialism on a qualitatively new basis, and that is on the basis of the latest and most advanced achievements of the scientific and technological revolution.*

The second problem concerns the development of the main productive force – man, who builds and puts into operation the material and technical base and without whose work the most perfect technology would be lifeless.

In its work for the formation and development of the new man, the worker of socialism and the future builder of communism, the Party takes into account first of all the changes taking place within the working class, within the classes of the cooperative farmers and the intelligentsia, and also the inter-class changes which in their totality lead to the *gradual creation of a socially homogeneous society.* And social homogeneity is a sine qua non for the richness of human nature. This process is an expression of one of the basic laws of the construction and development of mature socialism and the transition to communism.

We will continue to pay the greatest attention to the changes that are to take place in the social nature, the character of labour, the conscience, mentality and behaviour of the builders of socialism as a result of the intensification of the economy, the improvement of the agro-industrial and industrial-agrarian complexes, the interpenetration and gradual merger of the two forms of socialist ownership, the development of education and culture. The Party will create conditions for the correct regulation of these class and social changes, for the establishment and promotion of *relations between the builders of socialism which are new in character*, relations of comradeship and cooperation, of collectivity and mutual assistance. These relations are not only a characteristic feature of socialism, they will not only continue to develop and be enriched in the process of our further advance towards communism, but are also a powerful factor in accelerating this process. In the course of the forward movement, the complex and historically significant *process of overcoming the essential differences between town and village, between manual and intellectual work,* will gradually be adjusted.

It is pointed out in the Party Programme that 'the overcoming of the class and social differences and the strengthening of the common features in the builders of socialism are two facets of the same process: the gradual shaping of a versatile personality.'

It is true that there still are certain citizens who, due to a number of circumstances are, to a greater or lesser degree, alien to the socialist consciousness.

But at the present stage, we can say with good reason that, as a result of the objective changes in society and the educational activity of the Party, *the socialist personality is the predominant type of personality in the country.* At the same time, however, the general cultural standards of people are not yet up to the necessary level and there are often features in their morality and behaviour which run counter to the requirements of socialism. That is why we now face the practical task of involving all working people, and the younger generation in particular, in the process of moulding the socialist personality and its many-sided development, of waging a struggle against the vestiges of the past in people's views and behaviour.

Most important in this process is *to step up the social*

activity of the builder of socialism and especially his creative participation in labour, and in producing new material and spiritual wealth. In this particular sphere, the attitude to labour, there is still much to be desired. For example, we can in no way be satisfied with the present state of *discipline.* Labour, planning, contractual and finance discipline continues to be violated and leniency and mistaken liberalism are shown towards the offenders. The question of discipline is not simply an economic problem. It reveals the degree which the development of the socialist personality has attained, the level of its consciousness and sense of responsibility before itself and society and, in the final count, its attitude towards the socialist system.

The same holds good of *the attitude towards socialist ownership.* Socialist ownership is the basis on which the material and spiritual values of the socialist society are created and multiplied, the new relations between people, relations of comradely cooperation and mutual assistance, are built. It is the result of the concerted efforts and hard work of the working people from town to village, free from exploitation. *Socialist ownership is the ultimate basis of the socialist social system.* Along the way of its development and improvement of the ever closer rapprochement and merger of state and cooperative ownership, it turns into unified socialist ownership, and then gradually evolves into communist ownership. This is an objective law, and it is our duty to create the most favourable conditions for its manifestation.

It is for this reason that the Party and the state, the builders of socialism devote and should devote the greatest care to the consolidation and development of the national and cooperative forms of socialist ownership, to raising their level and their steady improvement. At the same time this obliges us to tolerate no manifestations of squandering socialist property, of encroachment on it, which unfortunately occur in our country. It is no secret that there are such cases at enterprises and agro-industrial complexes, in construction and also in the services. Certain individuals do harm to the national wealth out of neglect and carelessness, while others, from criminal motives, make a grab for the fruits of the people's work. These acts are incompatible with socialist morality and the laws of the socialist community, they do harm both to the public and the personal interests of the builders of socialism. They must be resolutely discontinued and eradicated. *Socialist ownership in its two forms is sacred and inviolable. It is all people's wealth.*

The building of developed socialism and the gradual transition to communism demand from *each able-bodied member of society to work according to his knowledge and abilities, to raise labour productivity, to fulfil consciously and creatively the tasks assigned to him.* In this connection it is necessary to continue to perfect the use of *material and moral incentives* and to combine them correctly. The classics of Marxism have made it clear that work under socialism is remunerated and the growing needs of the people are met on the basis of the *socialist principle of distribution: 'From everyone according to his abilities, to everyone according to his work'.* The quantity and quality of the work done is and should be the main yardstick in determining the working wage, the incomes of the working people.

Parallel with this *the social consumption funds* will continue to grow in keeping with the development of the productive forces and the rise in labour productivity, with the increase of the public wealth.

The socialist principle of distribution will continue to play a major role under mature socialism and the transition to communism, i.e. until it plays itself out, or in other words – until objective and subjective conditions are created for adopting *the communist principle: 'From everyone according to his abilities, to everyone according to this needs'*. However, a long period of time is necessary to achieve this, during which the material and technical base of communism will be built, a classless society will be created, the production relations will be formed on the basis of the unified communist ownership, and work for the welfare of society will become a primary vital need, a conscious necessity. Marx pointed out that 'The relations of distribution correspond to historically determined, specific social forms of the process of production and of those relations in which people enter in the process of reproducing their human life, and are the result of the above-mentioned forms and relations. (K. Marx, F. Engels, Works, Vol. 25, part two, p. 428, Bulgarian edition). This means that the communist mode of production will be matched by a corresponding communist principle of distribution.

The eradication of bourgeois vestiges in the morality, consciousness and behaviour of the workers of socialism, in our socialist reality, is a task of tremendous importance for the development of mature socialism and the creation of conditions for the gradual transition to the highest stage of communism. The many-sided development of the individual is organically linked with the necessity to further unfold the struggle against negative phenomena in our life.

Naturally, the positive qualitative and quantitative changes inside the country and on the international arena will further restrict and eliminate the conditions for the appearance and ımanifestation in our country of views and acts alien to socialism, and the possibility of infiltration of bourgeois influences from outside will be narrowed. However, the struggle against the survivals of the past is not a random process. It requires the active and uncompromising participation of the subjective factor. It is at the same time a struggle for the spreading and establishment of the socialist virtues, for the strengthening and development of the most valuable qualities of socialism, for the spiritual uplift of the builders of socialism.

The third problem is related to the necessity of broadly unfolding criticism and self-criticism in our society as a whole.

Criticism and self-criticism are objective laws of socialist development. Under socialism, they develop in the conditions of a non-antagonistic social structure of society, unity of the vital interests of all classes and groups on the basis of the historic goals of the working class. This makes criticism and self-criticism a necessary and effective means of pinpointing on time the emerging problems, of reassessing the obsolescent forms and mechanism in public life, of rejecting the outdated and stimulating the new, of combating deviations from the socialist norms. Marx pointed out that the proletarian revolutions, in contrast to all preceding revolutions, 'are constantly criticizing themselves.' (K. Marx, F. Engels, Works, Vol. 8, p. 120). *The socialist society cannot be renovated without criticizing itself.* That is why the degree of development of criticism and self-criticism is a criterion of the maturity of the socialist society itself.

Formulating the task of creating conditions for the unfolding of this objective law, which is to play an ever more important role during the transition to communism, the Party reminds us that *criticism and self-criticism in all spheres of public life will be only as good as they are in the Party organizations.* What is more, it is necessary to realize that without the initiative, the example and all-round support on the part of the leading organs, no criticism or self-criticism is possible.

In this respect the mass media are of tremendous significance. They should be granted much greater rights to criticize and should, on their part, require replies and practical action from those who are being criticized. Naturally, we have in mind criticism which is made on the basis of completely genuine facts and in the spirit of the Party policy.

The fourth problem to which the Party will devote a growing attention is the expansion and deepening of our integration with the fraternal socialist countries, the consistent application of the policy of all-round rapprochement between the People's Republic of Bulgaria and the Union of the Soviet Socialist Republics.

As a manifestation of the historic process of internationalization of production, socialist integration has the character of an objective law in the building of mature socialism and the gradual transition to communism. The accelerated progress of the country is not possible without the development and deepening of integration with the socialist countries and, above all, with the Soviet Union.

The greater the successes achieved in the development of the productive forces and in scientific and technological progress in the countries of the socialist community, the more imperative the natural necessity for integration becomes. At the same time, increasingly favourable conditions are being created for its actual and most consistent realization. In this respect the role of the conscientious and purposeful work of the Marxist-Leninist parties in the socialist countries is extremely great. In our opinion, the elaboration and coordination of the long-term strategy of the socio-economic policy of the CMEA member-states, which will reflect the principal trends in every country and in the community as a whole, is assuming great significance at the present stage.

The process of all-round rapprochement and integration with the Soviet Union, of deepening cooperation and integration links with the other socialist countries is an important factor in raising labour productivity and the effectiveness of the economy. This process faces us with important theoretical and practical problems, relating to the management of the national economy, to the establishment of synchronized normative systems, to the content of educational work. We expect from our scientists, from the specialists in this sphere, new theoretical studies which will give an answer to the problems arising from the development of integration, which will generalize on the basis of the experience that has been accumulated and will help the all-round unfolding of this objective process.

The fifth problem concerns the class and Party patriotic and internationalist education of the people and the youth.

The objective processes which are underway in the life of the country and of the world socialist community create conditions for and lead to qualitative changes in the content of both patriotism and internationalism.

Today our patriotism is not simply love for the homeland, but love for the *socialist homeland,* for *socialist* Bulgaria, i.e. it is *socialist patriotism,* which organically contains both the communist ideology and the internationalism that stems from it.

Internationalism has undergone and is now undergoing qualitative changes. After the emergence of the revolutionary workers' movement, *internationalism assumed definite class character,* clearly formulated in the famous slogan of the Communist Manifesto: 'Workers of the world, unite!' After the victory of the October Revolution, proletarian internationalism assumed as its characteristic feature *fraternal solidarity with the Soviet Union* – the first state of the workers and peasants. 'A touchstone' – this is how Georgi Dimitrov described the attitude to the great country of Lenin – the hope of working mankind, the mainstay of the world revolutionary process.

The Second World War made further inroads into the world of capitalism. *Socialist internationalism as an expression of the common interests of the working class and the peoples of the countries with a socialist social system* emerged on the basis of proletarian internationalism.

The stepping up of socialist construction, of the integration processes in defence and the economy, in science and culture, in ideology and politics, strengthened and deepened the unity and cohesion of the member-countries of the Council for Mutual Economic Assistance and the Warsaw Treaty. In entering the stage of building a developed socialist society in our country especially after the adoption of the new Programme of the BCP, considerable changes appeared and developed in the patriotic and internationalist consciousness of our people, a *process was started of a gradual interpenetration and coalescence of socialist patriotism and socialist internationalism.*

This process is most clearly manifested in the attitude towards the Soviet Union — the historic nucleus around which crystallizes the socialist community. In the sphere of Bulgaro-Soviet relations, we can now definitely speak of a *qualitatively new patriotic and internationalist consciousness of the Bulgarian people, of the rise and establishment of a new type of patriotism, in which love for Bulgaria and love for the Soviet Union are mutually supplementing and enriching each other and are ever more merging into one feeling, into an integrated consciousness.*

The Bulgarian Communist Party will continue consistently and undeviatingly to strengthen the fraternal Bulgaro-Soviet friendship, the friendship and cooperation with the peoples of the socialist community, with the communists and all progressive forces in the world, it will mould in all Bulgarian citizens a highly developed class and Party patriotic and internationalist consciousness as one of the most characteristic features of the socialist personality.

Comrade delegates,

Such are the main results of the fulfilment of the decisions of the Tenth Party Congress, such are the principal problems and tasks that we are faced with in the further building of the developed socialist society.

Everything that has been achieved is the work of the heroic working class, of the selfless workers in agriculture, of the people's intelligentsia, the result of the tireless work of the hundreds of thousands of communists, of the millions of workers of socialism in town and village.

Everything that has been achieved is the result of the inviolable unity and fraternal cooperation with the great Soviet people, with the peoples from the countries of the world socialist community, the result of proletarian internationalism, of the unity and cohesion of the international communist and workers' movement, whose loyal detachment is the Bulgarian Communist Party.

In the days when we are celebrating the twentieth anniversary of the April Plenary Session of the CC of the BCP, a historic event for the Party and the country, and are casting a glance at what has been done since, we can express deep satisfaction with the road which has been traversed. The fruitful results that have been attained in all spheres of our socio-political, economic and cultural development confirmed unconditionally the correctness and vitality of the April policy of the Party. This policy, a Leninist policy, a creative policy, is further elaborated and embodied in the Party Programme, approved by the Tenth Congress.

The present Eleventh Party Congress is called upon

to elaborate the programme and, in its spirit, to formulate the tasks for the period that follows. The fulfilment of these tasks will bring us still closer to the immediate historic goal of the Bulgarian Communist Party. While this path is being traversed, in the depths of our socialist society there will emerge and strengthen more and more elements characteristic of the communist phase, and the prerequisites for a gradual transition to the building of communism will be established and unfolded. There is no impenetrable wall, no social vacuum between the further development of socialism and the building of communism. This is an integral continuous process, a law-governed transition from the lower to the higher phase of the communist society. Evidently, the specific problems of this transition will be the subject of the future congresses of our Party.

Comrades,

The awareness that now we are not only building developed socialism, that we are not only raising the people's living standards, but we are also creating more and more material and cultural prerequisites for a wealthier and happier life of the coming generations who will build communism, multiplies our forces. This awareness is a powerful stimulus in our further work and struggle for the realization of the plans mapped out by the Party.

From the Congress rostrum I urge you all, dear comrades, the Party organizations and all members of the glorious Bulgarian Communist Party, our loyal allies – the agrarians, all builders of socialism in our dear Fatherland, to tireless constructive work for the fulfilment of the decisions of the Eleventh Party Congress, for the good of the people, in the name of our glorious and immortal communist ideal!

Long live the heroic Party of the Bulgarian communists, boundlessly loyal to Marxism-Leninism and proletarian internationalism!

Long live the Bulgarian people – selfless builders of the developed socialist society!

Long live the great Soviet Union and its militant vanguard – the Communist Party of the Soviet Union, the standard-bearer of our epoch!

Long live and grow strong the unity and friendship of the peoples of the socialist community, of the great army of communists in the world, of all forces fighting for peace, freedom, democracy and social progress!

May our victorious Marxist-Leninist teaching live through the ages!

Long live communism!

TODOR ZHIVKOV

Closing Remarks

Comrades,

A total of 105 delegations of communist and workers' parties, of socialist and national-democratic parties, organizations and movements took part as guests in the work of the Eleventh Congress of our Party. It is a great honour to us that they took up our invitation.

I believe that I shall be voicing the thoughts of the delegates to the Congress, of all Bulgarian communists, when I assure you, esteemed guests, that the Bulgarian Communist Party, the Party of Dimiter Blagoev and Georgi Dimitrov, will always be unshakably loyal to Marxism-Leninism and proletarian internationalism, will always march in the militant ranks of the world communist and workers movement, will support the just cause of the national-liberation movements, will take an active part, together with all honest people the world over, in the struggle for peace, freedom and independence, for democracy and social progress.

Dear comrades, please convey to your parties and peoples the fraternal greetings of the Bulgarian communists, of the entire Bulgarian people. We wholeheartedly wish you fresh successes and achievements in your work and struggle for the happiness and well-being of your peoples, for the happiness and progress of mankind.

The Party congresses have always been exceptional

events in its life, they have always exerted a tremendous influence on the destinies of the people, on the country's sociopolitical, economic and cultural development. It is precisely for this reason that the work of the present Congress has been followed with such great attention by the communists, by the entire people.

As you know, the work of the Eleventh Congress, its sessions were broadcast by Bulgarian Television and Radio and were given wide coverage in the press. In this way all Bulgarian communists, all Bulgarian citizens became participants in the Congress. We are fully justified to state: the Eleventh Congress has entered every Bulgarian home.

Friends and comrades-in-arms from near and distant countries, all who are interested in the activity of the Bulgarian communists, in the life of the Bulgarian people had ample opportunity to get acquainted with the work of the Congress.

The Bulgarian Communist Party has no secrets from its people. This precisely is one of the secrets of our successes.

Our Party is a living part of the Bulgarian people, its universally acknowledged and beloved leader. The Bulgarian people are politically mature. Under the leadership of the Party they passed with honour the severe test of the struggle against fascism and capitalism. Under the leadership of the Party they performed miracles in the building of the new life. Under the leadership of the Party they have reached the highest peak in their 13-centuries-long history.

Party and people have really merged in Bulgaria in inseparable unity. There is no power in this world, either internal or external, which can break this unity, which can impair the Party's loyalty to its people, the people's

138

faith in their Party! And it is not only a poetic image when we say that the once lonely red poppy is now blossoming all over the country, that contemporary Bulgaria is red in every drop of blood of its people.

Our Party does not have and cannot have any secrets from such a people!

Nor do we have any secrets from our comrades, friends and co-workers throughout the world.

Some may say: all this is true; but was it right, along with our great successes, to show before the whole world our difficulties, our weaknesses and shortcomings?

We are aware that some people somewhere will try to exploit our criticism and self-criticism, to exaggerate the weaknesses and shortcomings, to denigrate our Party and our people. But we are also aware that they have always fed on the crumbs from our dining table.

As regards our Party, it has never feared the shrill cries and the slander of the enemies. One of the sources of its strength is that it sees not only the successes, but the weaknesses and shortcomings as well, that it itself wages a battle against them and rouses the people in the struggle to overcome them.

The Eleventh Congress has impressively shown what remarkable successes we have scored in the economy and in cultural development, in the promotion of socialist democracy, in the establishment of the socialist lifestyle. I am convinced that not only we, in this hall, but all who have followed our sessions, have felt the Marxist-Leninist maturity with which the Congress assessed the achievements of the Sixth Five-Year Plan and in the spirit of the April policy, in the spirit of the Party Programme, mapped out and discussed the tasks of the next period.

It is no accident that the Eleventh Congress reverberated so widely among the working class, among the working people in agriculture, among our intelligentsia, among the women and the youth, among the Bulgarian people.

Our socialist country, comrades, has excellent acoustics! The Party's truthful and inspired words are heard in all corners of our land, they resound in the hearts and minds of all people. And all strata of the population have found a way of expressing their full support to what has been said in this hall.

This shows once again that the Bulgarian Communist Party correctly expresses the vital interests of the people, that it correctly maps out the roads and puts on them the signs pointing to the immediate historical task—the building of a developed socialist society and the preparation for the gradual transition to communism in our dear fatherland—the People's Republic of Bulgaria.

Comrades,

There is no doubt that now for us, the delegates to the Congress, for all communists, the main task is the fulfillment of the Congress decisions. The Seventh Five-Year Plan is realistic but demanding. The five-year period should become a period of great efficiency and high quality. Many efforts will be needed to implement the guidelines for the development of the economy and scientific and technological progress, for raising the people's material well-being and culture.

These are really great problems. But if we say that these problems are the main thing that now moves us—this will be true, without being all.

We, the delegates to the Congress, the communists, are no less moved by the confidence of our people in us, in our Party, a confidence which was so clearly manifested during the days of the Congress. Without exaggeration we can declare that the entire work of the Congress was aimed at this: to justify the trust of the Party, the trust of the people.

Now, at the end of the Congress, we are preoccupied with the thought of how, through our work to implement the decisions of the Congress, through our all-round activities, we, our Party, might best live up to the confidence of the people and their faith in us, to the hopes which our people pin on the Bulgarian Communist Party.

We leave the Congress with the feeling of victors, and not only we, the delegates, not only we, the Bulgarian communists; the whole Bulgarian people leaves the Congress as a victor who, guided and led by its Communist Party, will turn the Congress decisions into a material force, into a living reality.

That is why we address the last words spoken from this rostrum, words of gratitude and affection, words of appeal for new deeds, to our heroic working class, to our selfless workers in agriculture, to the intelligentsia, loyal to communism, to the glorious Bulgarian women, to the ardent Bulgarian youth and its Dimitrov Komsomol.

Let us honour the people—creators of all material and cultural wealth, the people, flesh of whose flesh and blood is our own Bulgarian Communist Party!

Notes

The following definitions are designed to clarify the meaning of some probably unfamiliar terms which occur in Todor Zhivkovs's remarks.

April Policy—The political course endorsed by the April 1956 Plenum of the Central Committee of the BCP, developed and elaborated at subsequent Party congresses and plenary sessions. The April 1956 Plenum ". . . fully restored the Leninist principles of leadership and norms of Party life, bringing the Party's constructive work wholly into line with the requirements of the objective laws of social developments. . ." (Program of the BCP, 1971, p. 6)

The April Policy provided the conditions for extensively developing the Party's and the people's creative initiative, for securing the greatest success in economic and cultural construction, development of social relations, expansion of socialist democracy and improvement of the people's living standards. The effectiveness of the April policy was clearly demonstrated in the decisions of the Tenth Party Congress (1971) which adopted a program for construction of a developed socialist society, a program which continued and developed the course established in 1956.

Fatherland Front—The largest sociopolitical organization in the People's Republic of Bulgaria, bringing together in unity the workers, working people, farmers and intellectuals, under the leadership of the BCP. The Fatherland Front is the link between the Party and non-Party people, and the broadest social support of the people's power.

National Assembly—Supreme organ of state power in the People's Republic of Bulgaria, consisting of 400 representatives elected on the basis of universal suffrage, by secret ballot, for a five-year term. The National Assembly represents the Bulgarian people and exercises all rights ensuing from their sovereignty.

State Council—Supreme, continuously functioning body of state power which both adopts and implements decisions. Elected by and responsible to the National Assembly, it consists of a president, deputy presidents, a secretary and members, all elected from among the national representatives.

At its first session on July 8, 1971, the Sixth National Assembly elected the State Council with its president, Todor Zhivkov, a first deputy president, three deputy presidents, a secretary, and seventeen members.

People's Councils—Organs of state power and people's self-government at the municipal, district and regional levels. The members of the People's Councils are guided in their activity by common national interests, the interests of the people of their districts and regions, as well as the concerns of the people living in their electoral areas.

Personal Plots—In the People's Republic of Bulgaria the means of production are owned by the whole people. This, however, does not preclude individual property, including certain means of production owned by citizens. This is *personal* rather than *private* property. A person who owns a piece of land, or a lathe, must farm or operate it himself, and may not hire someone else to do so.